OECD Health Policy Studies

Achieving Better Value for Money in Health Care

OECD

ORGANISATION FOR ECONOMIC CO-OPERATION AND DEVELOPMENT

The OECD is a unique forum where the governments of 30 democracies work together to address the economic, social and environmental challenges of globalisation. The OECD is also at the forefront of efforts to understand and to help governments respond to new developments and concerns, such as corporate governance, the information economy and the challenges of an ageing population. The Organisation provides a setting where governments can compare policy experiences, seek answers to common problems, identify good practice and work to co-ordinate domestic and international policies.

The OECD member countries are: Australia, Austria, Belgium, Canada, the Czech Republic, Denmark, Finland, France, Germany, Greece, Hungary, Iceland, Ireland, Italy, Japan, Korea, Luxembourg, Mexico, the Netherlands, New Zealand, Norway, Poland, Portugal, the Slovak Republic, Spain, Sweden, Switzerland, Turkey, the United Kingdom and the United States. The Commission of the European Communities takes part in the work of the OECD.

OECD Publishing disseminates widely the results of the Organisation's statistics gathering and research on economic, social and environmental issues, as well as the conventions, guidelines and standards agreed by its members.

This document has been produced with the financial assistance of the European Union. The views expressed herein can in no way be taken to reflect the official opinion of the European Union.

ISBN 978-92-64-07420-0 (print)
ISBN 978-92-64-07423-1 (PDF)

Series: *OECD Health Policy Studies*
ISSN 2074-3181 (print)
ISSN 2074-319X (online)

Also available in French: *Obtenir un meilleur rapport qualité-prix dans les soins de santé*

Corrigenda to OECD publications may be found on line at: *www.oecd.org/publishing/corrigenda*.

Foreword

All OECD and European Union members are facing problems of financing their health systems. Total spending on health care has risen from an average of around 7% in 1990 to almost 9% in 2006. The public component of health care spending has been rising in step and this is placing increasing pressure on public sector budgets. Rising expectations of high-quality care in a period of ageing populations and rapid technological change suggest that upward financial pressure on health systems will remain for some time to come. In this context, member countries of the two organisations have emphasised the need for achieving better value for money in health systems as one means of offsetting some of the fiscal stress.

In the light of this, a one-day conference was organised by the European Commission and the OECD on 17 September 2008 in Brussels. The conference was entitled "Improving Health System Efficiency: Achieving Better Value for Money", reflecting the interest in both organisations about improving the performance and functioning of the health care systems.

This volume begins with an introductory overview of the presentations to the conference and the ensuing discussions. It is followed by a context-setting chapter that examines some of the recent developments in spending and attempts to unravel some of the possible reasons for the wide cross-country differences in health spending relative to GDP.

The remainder contains an assessment of five policy areas which countries may wish to review: the role of competition in health markets; the scope for improving care coordination policies; the potential benefits of better pharmaceutical pricing policies; the need for greater quality control supported by strengthened ICT policies; and, the costs and benefits of increased cost-sharing. The chapters aim at providing summaries of existing policies (with their strengths and weaknesses), available information on their impacts and, to the extent possible, a checklist of potential policy levers in each of these areas.

While the chapters and the conference discussions suggest a range of avenues for exploration, policies will need careful design and adaptation to national arrangements so as to avoid undesired side-effects that may compromise wider other health system objectives. More generally, the use of multiple instruments may help ensure the achievement of as wide a range of health care objectives as possible.

This report is a joint product co-financed by the European Commission (DGEMPL) and the OECD.

The authors of the chapters in this report – David Morgan, Howard Oxley, Elizabeth Docteur, Valerie Paris, Nicolaas Klazinga and Elettra Ronchi – are all of the OECD Health Division, and Peter C. Smith is Professor at the Imperial College Business School (London).

Howard Oxley and Elizabeth Docteur (formerly of the OECD Health Division) provided oversight and support in the initial preparation of the papers. Anne Schwartz helped in the drafting of the introductory chapter. Statistical and secretarial supports were provided by Rie Fujisawa, Elena Rusticelli and Judy Zinnemann.

Finally thanks also goes to Ana Xavier and the other members of the European Commission for the organisation of the conference held on 17 September 2008 in Brussels when the papers were first presented as well as to the numerous members of the Health Division and the European Commission and other conference participants who commented on the various chapters before, during and after the conference.

This publication is supported by the European Community Programme for Employment and Social Solidarity (2007-2013).

Table of Contents

Tables

Figures

Boxes

Introduction

The six chapters in this volume were prepared for a one-day conference, "Improving Health System Efficiency: Achieving Better Value for Money", held on 17 September 2008 in Brussels. Jointly organised by the European Commission and the OECD, the purpose of the conference was to assess policies leading to more rational use of resources in the health care sector and the potential of such policies to promote long-term sustainability of health systems. Attendees included officials of the two hosting institutions and other international organisations, representatives of their member countries who hold policy-setting positions and technical experts.

Both organisations have emphasised that health-care systems are coming under pressure due to rising expectations for high-quality care in a period of population ageing and rapid technological change. Member countries of the OECD and of the European Union have highlighted the need for better value for money in health systems during the deliberations of the OECD Health Committee and through the European Commission's Open Method of Co-ordination (OMC) on Social Protection and Social Inclusion.[1] The September 2008 meeting drew on the experiences of both organisations. In case of the European Union, a wide range of policies to encourage more rational resource use were identified in the 2006 National Strategy Reports and the 2007 Joint Report on Social Protection and Social Inclusion (European Commission, 2007).[2] These included: strengthening primary care provision and referral systems to secondary care; shifting care to an outpatient basis; increasing the productivity and quality of inpatient care; improving care co-ordination, improving incentives in payment systems and greater use of information and communications technologies (ICT) and e-health solutions. The OECD has been conducting in depth policy work on strategies for improving the performance of health-care systems, focusing on, among other things, care co-ordination, pharmaceutical pricing, and health information systems and information and ICT.[3]

Policy questions

Absolute growth in health expenditure and its growth in relation to national income raise the difficult question of whether and how to constrain it. Can systems become more efficient in how they spend their money? Where can savings be achieved without doing harm to the health of people in need of care, for example by reducing access to health care? As technological advances change the very nature of health care delivery, policy makers face difficult decisions about the additional expense associated with new life saving and life enhancing therapeutic agents, vaccines, imaging, and surgical techniques. How do the potential advances in health status and health services delivery weigh against the additional strain on societal resources?

The key policy question is "How can health systems improve efficiency of resource use and, thereby, help ensure the financial sustainability of health care systems?" In considering the policy approach most appropriate in any country, policy makers can benefit from a clear articulation of the problem, the potential solutions, the trade-offs they must make in pursuing various goals and the experiences of other countries. Thus, one important aim of the conference was to help policy makers as they grapple with these issues by identifying a checklist of policies or good practices worthy of consideration by national administrations. The six chapters in this volume provide analyses of multinational datasets, case studies of policy innovations, and discussion of both the challenges and opportunities to enhance value for money.

Unraveling cross national differences in health expenditures

In Chapter 1, "Patterns of Health Care Spending Growth", David Morgan and Howard Oxley of the OECD set the context for the chapters that follow. Drawing on the most recent OECD data, the chapter summarises trends in health expenditure among OECD countries since 1995. The authors note that, while growth in health spending was slow in the early part of the 1990s, the latter half of the decade was marked by strong growth in overall health spending across OECD countries, with health expenditure outstripping economic growth by almost two to one. Since 2003, this growth has abated but it remains unclear whether this is a temporary phenomenon or the beginning of a new trend. As of 2006, average health spending among OECD countries amounted to 9 % of GDP, up from just over 5% in 1970 and around 7% in 1990.

The chapter also looks at the components of growth and documents the substantial differences across OECD countries in expenditure, prices, volume, and types of services. For example, ten OECD countries spend more than 10% of GDP on health goods and services, including (in descending order) the United States, Switzerland, France, and Germany. By contrast, the Czech Republic, Korea, Mexico, Poland, and Turkey spend less than 7%.

A significant portion of the chapter focuses on the potential reasons for cross country variation, searching, in effect, for clues about areas that appear most promising for policy intervention As they note, "although the research evidence is not conclusive, policy makers still must make choices in their search for improved performance, focusing on either demand or supply related factors, or a combination of both." The chapter assembles a vast array of data on both demand and supply factors, ranging from national income, age distribution, and disease prevalence to the supply of health care professionals, remuneration of professionals, and the intensity of care and technological capacity. For example, an exploratory study in ten OECD countries of hospital costs associated with several conditions found wide variations and suggested that, on average, if unit costs were reduced to the level of the best performers, average costs could potentially be reduced by 5% and 48%. Similarly, data on the number of cardio-vascular procedures performed show the United States at twice the OECD average. By contrast, the rate in Switzerland is less than half the OECD average.

Market mechanisms: promise and limitations

In Chapter 2, "Market Mechanisms and the Use of Health Care Resources", Peter C. Smith of the Imperial College Business School (London) considers whether market mechanisms can lead to more rational use of health care resources. Smith points out the many ways in which the market for health care services departs from the neoclassical model, including the lack of information for consumers to make choices about care, the role of physicians and other professionals acting as agents for consumers, constraints on exit and entry into the market, financing of education and research as public goods, and the fact that patients rarely bear the full cost of the care they receive. But he also notes that "sole reliance on non-market mechanisms, such as the public sector, also gives rise to serious problems…There are unclear lines of accountability, between patients, providers, governments, taxpayers, and provider institutions such as hospitals, that offer enormous opportunities for opportunistic behaviour and inefficiency." The issue for policy makers thus is not whether markets are good or bad, but determining whether fostering some aspects of competition and markets in the health sector can lead to more rational use of resources, and which aspects of competition have the greatest potential to get results.

Smith examines the research evidence from experience with markets and competition to date. The chapter analyses three types of competition that give rise to quite different sets of incentives: competition for health insurance, competition for collectively purchased health services, and competition for individual patients. He points to a number of findings from the research literature that may be useful to policy makers, for example that provider markets respond to the priorities of purchasers, the choice of services that are the subject of competition have profound implications for system performance, and providers are responsive to payment incentives. He also offers some words of caution about the impact of provider competition for individual patients on cost competition. He concludes with some insights on policy designs that could take advantage of the power of markets while mitigating some of their more damaging effects. For example, Smith notes that pursuing competition in insurance requires creation of both risk sharing arrangements (to discourage cream skimming) as well as processes for quality assurance. He notes, however, that creating incentives for insurers to undertake long-term activities to foster population health outcomes may prove difficult, suggesting that such responsibilities may be better left to governments. He is more optimistic about the potential of market forces to yield cost efficiencies if purchasers have the ability to contract selectively with providers.

Care co-ordination

In Chapter 3, "Improving Health Care System Performance through Better Co-ordination of Care," Howard Oxley (OECD) addresses the scope for improving cost efficiency and quality of care through better care co-ordination, issues that are particularly important given the growing number of individuals living with chronic disease and the elderly who may have difficulty navigating fragmented health care systems or who are in need of long-term institutional care. Co-ordination problems can happen throughout health systems but most particularly at the barriers between primary, specialist, acute inpatient and long-term care.

Oxley presents a broad overview of care co-ordination issues and approaches from OECD countries plus several other nations that are part of the European Union. Common themes include widespread concern about care co-ordination, the importance of policies affecting referrals, and the key role of primary care providers in managing care, even when the arrangements are not formal. Drawing on a survey to which 26 of these countries responded, he also identifies the key impediments to care co-ordination such as fragmented financing, limitations on different providers' scope of practice, and spanning levels of care. The chapter also examines whether targeted programmes, primarily those structured to provide disease or case management, can improve the quality and cost-efficiency or cost-effectiveness of health care systems. Oxley concludes by suggesting four key areas are critical for achieving improvements in care co-ordination and in overall system performance: improved information technology and communication infrastructure for information transfer; review of the adequacy of resources devoted to ambulatory and primary care; reconfiguring provider systems and incentives to enhance care co-ordination, and breaking down barriers between levels and components of care. Discussion at the September 2008 conference noted the need for policy makers to carefully consider culture, history, and specific aspects of system design when making reforms to improve care co-ordination.

Pharmaceutical policy: finding the right balance

Although accounting for a relatively small portion of health expenditure for OECD countries, spending on pharmaceuticals is growing at an average annual rate of 5.7%, outstripping growth both for other types of health care and gross domestic product (GDP). Policy makers are thus increasingly concerned about pricing and reimbursement policies for drugs. In Chapter 4, "Ensuring Efficiency in Pharmaceutical Expenditures", Elizabeth Docteur and Valerie Paris of the OECD explore options as to how to structure these policies to promote cost efficiency. The global nature of the pharmaceutical industry, however, creates special concerns since policies in one country can have repercussions in others.

Policy making with respect to pharmaceuticals must deal with the twin objectives of promoting innovation in drug development while also securing the best possible price for consumers and payers. As they note, "perhaps the most difficult trade-off in pharmaceutical policy is that between static efficiency (maximising consumer welfare by getting the most health value from today's expenditures constrained by the limits of present technological capability) and dynamic efficiency (creating incentives for research and development of products that improve capacity to prevent health conditions and cure diseases in the future)." An additional concern is whether the distribution system, which can account for a third or more of the retail price, is functioning efficiently.

Docteur and Paris provide an overview of current policies related to coverage, pricing, and other techniques to influence the demand and mix of pharmaceuticals. The section on pricing is particularly rich, sketching the variation across OECD countries in the use of external benchmarking, internal reference pricing, pricing using pharmaco-economic assessment, price-volume agreements, and risk-sharing regimes. They also offer a menu of options for reforming policies including changes in reimbursement and pricing, increasing the role of pharmaco-economic assessment in determining value for expenditure, steering demand towards products of greatest value, and providing incentives for more efficient distribution mechanisms. The chapter concludes with a checklist to guide policy makers as they grapple with these issues. For example, the authors suggest that policy makers should:

- consider relative cost-effectiveness in pricing and purchasing decisions, while ensuring that rewards to innovation are consistent with the value of benefits offered;
- seek opportunities for establishing price-volume agreements or confidential rebates when value-based prices cannot be established;
- explore using risk-sharing arrangements to reduce the financial risk presented by new medicines when information on their cost and their expected effect on health outcomes is insufficient;
- encourage generic substitution and price competition in the off-patent market;
- create incentives for appropriate prescribing, dispensing and use of medicines;
- consider whether there are opportunities for efficiencies in the distribution chain; and,
- ensure that overall health care spending efficiency is not compromised by efforts to improve efficiency of pharmaceutical expenditure.

Improving data systems to promote quality of care

In Chapter 5, "Using ICT to Monitor and Improve Quality in Health Care", Nicolaas Klazinga and Elettra Ronchi of the OECD focus on a key strategy for enhancing value for money: improving the quality of health care services. Although there is controversy regarding the accuracy of available estimates, they comment, "there is, today, general agreement that quality problems are likely to have a significant health and economic impact in OECD countries." Quality improvement through greater ICT use offers the promise of both reducing system waste (by eliminating the use of unnecessary services) and leading to real improvements in population health. Their chapter looks at the potential for increasing use of ICT at all levels of health-care system to monitor service delivery and patient outcomes and to facilitate changes in system design that will enhance the technical quality of care and patient satisfaction.

Klazinga and Ronchi note that improvements in the transmission of medical information – from patient to provider, among providers, and from provider to payer – have the potential to improve care co-ordination, reduce delivery of duplicative services, reduce administrative costs, give feedback to providers, and provide the basis for better planning and system enhancements. Their chapter describes the data sources that can be applied to quality improvement and outlines several of the strategies that have been implemented in OECD countries, focusing particular attention on the so-called pay-for-performance programmes in the United States and the United Kingdom. Special attention is also given to an innovative program in the Canadian province of British Columbia to monitor prescription drug use.

Klazinga and Ronchi are optimistic about the adoption of ICT more broadly throughout health care systems. Yet, information technology is capital intensive and costs of creating new systems and maintaining them over time must be balanced against purported gains. Key issues to be addressed include facilitating interoperability, the ability of different data systems to connect with each other via common data definitions and unique patient identifiers. Interoperability concerns also affect the ability of researchers to provide policy makers with reliable cross-country comparisons. The authors also note the importance of addressing privacy concerns head on, commenting that "although health care organisations have a strong interest in maintaining privacy and security, they must also balance this interest against the need to ensure that information can be retrieved easily when required for care." They further note that "the main challenge for decision makers is creating a smooth interface between privacy policy, legislation and technological requirements."

Discussion at the conference focused on the considerable challenges in securing resources for data systems and ensuring that data are entered reliably and accurately at the patient level. Given the level of investment and the desirability of making comparisons across systems, participants raised the potential for international co-operation involving OECD, the World Health Organisation, and the European Commission.

Understanding the effects of user charges

Finally, in Chapter 6 on "The Impact of User Charges in Health Care", Peter C. Smith of Imperial College Business School (London) examines the impact of user charges on utilisation, spending, and outcomes. Smith notes the dual purposes of imposing user charges: to finance the health system, and to influence the care-seeking behaviour of patients when there is no direct price to them (other than through the tax system or social contributions) for access to health care. In most developed nations, user charges are primarily intended to mitigate this problem of moral hazard. But does the research indicate that user charges actually result in the intended effects of reducing the use of services that are not necessarily needed?

Smith's chapter begins by examining the extent to which OECD countries currently rely on user charges in health care, describing recent policy innovations in Sweden, the Netherlands, Germany, and France, along with reference pricing techniques for drugs in the Slovak Republic.

The issue of whether current initiatives have proven effective in minimising frivolous use of health services that are not cost effective (and thus enhancing value of money) remains unknown. Important findings from the RAND health insurance experiment with variable levels of user charge in the United States, notable for its use of an experimental research design, indicated that higher user charges may lead to significant reductions in health care demand. Whilst this did not appear to affect the health status of most of the population, it did have severe health consequences for people with low incomes and chronic conditions. For example, when charges were imposed, poor control of hypertension resulted in an increase of the annual likelihood of death of approximately 10%.

Smith argues for a fundamental rethinking of user charges to ensure that their use is consistent with broader societal objectives, stating that: "The central policy problem is to decide which health care technologies should be subsidized from public funds. A policy of user charges then flows naturally from the choice of the subsidized treatments. Once the public package of care is chosen, patients would still be free to purchase the remaining unsubsidised interventions at market prices, or to purchase complementary private insurance to cover such interventions."

Policy makers will face difficult choices in their efforts to constrain health care growth and ensure that public expenditure is matched by commensurate benefits. The policies they choose to adopt will differ based on the characteristics of the health systems they administer. The analyses presented in this volume should help them understand the menu of policy options and the trade-offs implicit in their design, as well as the most current empirical knowledge about their use in other countries.

Notes

1. See *http://ec.europa.eu/employment_social/spsi/the_process_en.htm* for more information on the process.

2. See *http://ec.europa.eu/employment_social/spsi/joint_reports_en.htm* for the Joint Reports on Social Protection and Social Inclusion 2007 and *http://ec.europa.eu/employment_social/spsi/strategy_reports_en.htm* for the National Strategy Reports.

3. For a more complete description on the work conducted by the OECD, see *www.oecd.org/document/60/0,2340,en_2649_33929_37103164_1_1_1_1,0 0.html*

Chapter 1.

Patterns of Health Care Spending Growth

By Howard Oxley, formerly of the Health Division,
and David Morgan, Health Division, OECD

This chapter examines recent spending growth and the role of the underlying components of spending in these developments. It then looks at possible reasons for the wide variance in the level of health care spending across OECD and European countries.

Introduction

Health care spending has generally increased more rapidly than both gross domestic product (GDP) and per capita incomes in virtually all OECD countries. Spending on health goods and services now absorbs a large share of total resources in the economy and this share continues to grow. On average, total health care spending represented just under 9% of GDP by 2006 – up from just over 5% in 1970 and around 7% in 1990. Despite a recent slowdown in spending growth, the most recent OECD projections suggest that pressures on health care spending are likely to continue although the potential amount estimated depends on the specific assumptions used.[1]

Most countries are exploring ways to improve the performance of health care systems, among other things, by enhancing cost efficiency and effectiveness of care. Such efforts should improve the longer-term financial sustainability of health care systems, particularly in countries where expenditure spending is already high. But even lower-spending countries are examining policy alternatives to limit the rise in expenditure.

As a prelude to discussions of ways of improving efficiency, this chapter first examines spending growth and the major components of this growth over the past decade. It then looks at differences in expenditure levels across countries and considers possible reasons for the wide variance. This information may help countries determine where they should focus future policy attention. This chapter largely draws on *OECD Health Data* (OECD, 2007a; OECD, 2008) and *Health at a Glance* (OECD, 2007b).

Patterns of expenditure growth over the recent past

Growth in health care spending since 1995

Over the period 1995-2006, annual per capita health expenditure is estimated to have grown on average by a little more than 4% (Figure 1.1). Countries that experienced the highest growth over this period tended to be those that had relatively low health expenditure as a share of GDP in the mid-1990s, such as Ireland, Korea and Turkey, which had growth rates up to twice the OECD average over the period (Figure 1.2). Others, such as France, Germany, Japan and Switzerland, experienced only modest growth during this period, reflecting both cost-containment measures, and the impact of weaker growth in average incomes in these countries on the demand for care. Real per capita health spending in these countries in 2006 was only 20% to 30% higher than the levels in 1995, compared with an OECD-wide increase of over 50%.

Figure 1.1. Annual average growth rate in real health expenditure per capita, 1995-2006

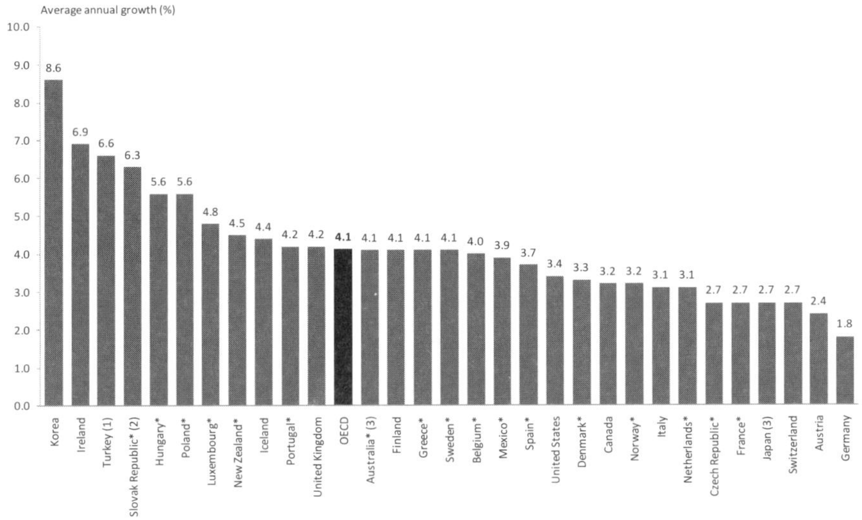

* Series breaks.

1. 1999-2005.

2. 1997-2005.

3. 1995-2005.

Source: OECD (2008), *OECD Health Data*.

Over this time frame, three different sub-periods can be identified (Figure 1.3). In the mid-1990s, health spending grew fairly slowly, at rates a little above that of overall economic growth. From the late 1990s until around 2003, overall health spending grew strongly across the OECD, with health expenditure outstripping economic growth by almost two to one. In the United States, despite some success in managing care by insurers during the 1990s, backlash from both consumers and providers against the most restrictive forms of managed care led insurers to loosen their interventions, resulting in renewed rapid cost growth. In some other countries, such as the United Kingdom, Canada, and Ireland, health spending growth reflected policies specifically aimed at increasing the level of public spending on health. Tight budgetary controls implemented in these countries during previous years had brought about constraints in capacity and surgical activity (Colombo and Morgan, 2006).

Figure 1.2. Health spending as share of gross domestic product, 1995 and per capita health expenditure growth, 1995 to 2006

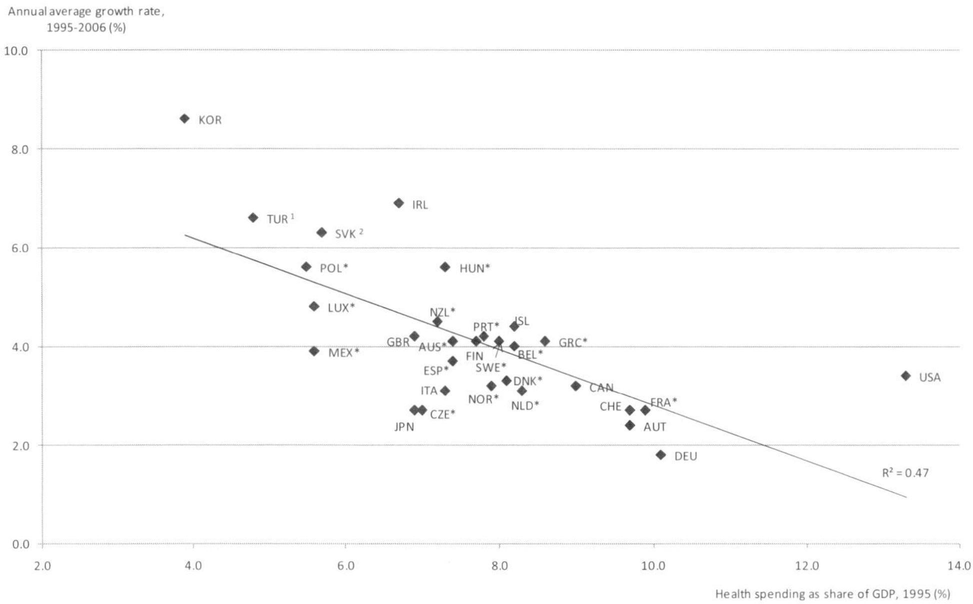

* Series break.

1. 1999-2005.

2. 1997-2005.

Source: OECD (2008), *OECD Health Data*.

More recent data for the three years up to 2006 show signs of a slowdown for the OECD average. Over this period, expenditure growth slowed to about the rates experienced during the mid-1990s and overall economic growth remained broadly unchanged. It remains to be seen whether this slowdown can be sustained. In the past, many policies aimed at controlling expenditure growth had only short- to medium-term effects and had to be supplemented by successive additional policy packages.[2]

Figure 1.3. Annual average growth rate in health expenditure and gross domestic product, 1995-2006

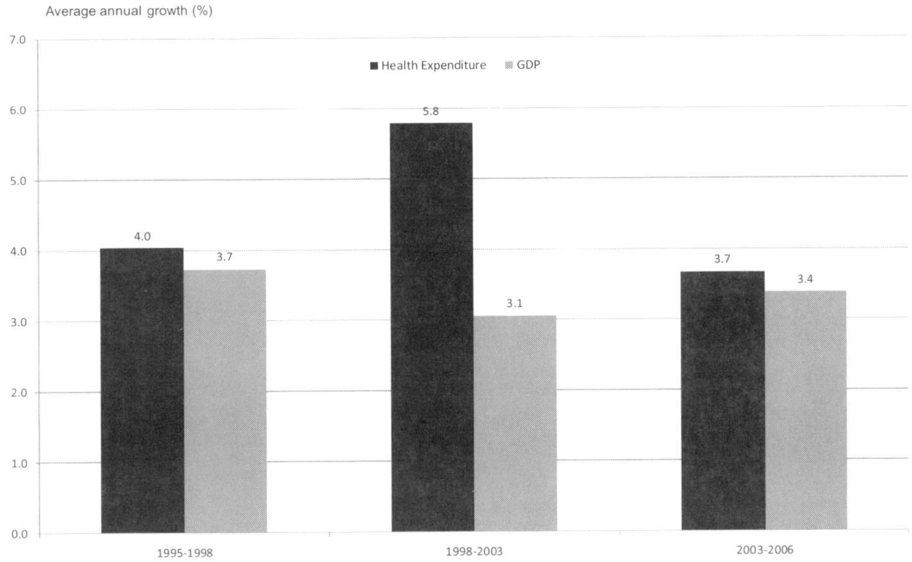

Source: OECD (2008), *OECD Health Data*.

Contributions to growth in spending

Spending on medical goods, and in particular pharmaceuticals, has risen rapidly across most OECD countries, consuming an increasing share of overall health expenditure. Since 1995, growth in pharmaceutical spending has averaged around 4.6%, compared with the 4.0% annual rise in total health spending. By 2006, pharmaceuticals accounted for around 17% of health spending or 1.5% of GDP. Yet, despite this rapid growth, medical goods has a smaller share of health spending compared with the other main two components of health spending (hospitals and ambulatory care), and its contribution to overall growth in health care spending was smaller over the period 1995 to 2006 (Figure 1.4). Overall across a group of OECD countries with consistent data, medical goods contributed to about one fifth of overall health spending growth, compared with over 60% from hospital and ambulatory providers.

Again, there is much variation across countries. In Canada, for example, albeit over a shorter period, medical goods have been the main driver of increasing health expenditure, contributing almost one-third. Around 30% of growth is also attributed to medical goods in France, Germany, and Japan. The ambulatory sector has contributed the most in Portugal, France, and the United States, explaining around 40% of overall health spending growth. This may reflect a continuing shift in care from inpatient to ambulatory care environments in these countries. Nonetheless, the hospital sector is the main contributor to growth overall: the Netherlands, Sweden and Turkey experienced significant contributions from the hospital sector with correspondingly low contributions from the ambulatory sector.[3]

Figure 1.4. Contribution to average annual growth rate in health expenditure per capita, 1995-2006

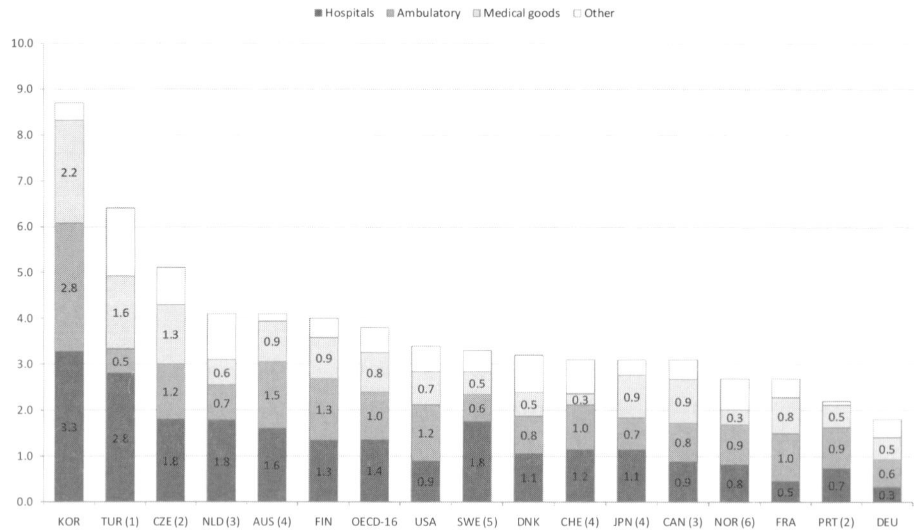

1. 1999-2005; 2. 2000-06; 3. 1998-2006; 4. 1995-2006; 5. 2001-06; 6. 1997-2005.

Source: OECD (2008), *OECD Health Data.*

The share of health-care spending in GDP

Overall, the share of GDP devoted to health care has increased over the past few decades. For a group of 24 OECD countries for which comparable historical series are available, this share has increased from an average of 6.6% in 1980 to 7.2% in 1990 and to 9.3% in 2006. But there is considerable variation across countries. The United States has consistently been the largest spender on health goods and services since 1980. The number of countries spending more than 10% of their GDP on health goods and services stood at eight in 2006, compared with four in 2000 and only two countries in 1995 (Figure 1.5). At the other extreme, the Czech Republic, Korea, Mexico, Poland, and Turkey spend less than 7%. This variation is even more marked on a per capita basis although these results do not take account of differences in average income (Figure 1.6). Nonetheless, there still appears to be substantial differences in per capita spending at similar income levels even after income is taken into account (Figure 1.7).

Figure 1.5. Total health expenditure as percentage of GDP, 2006

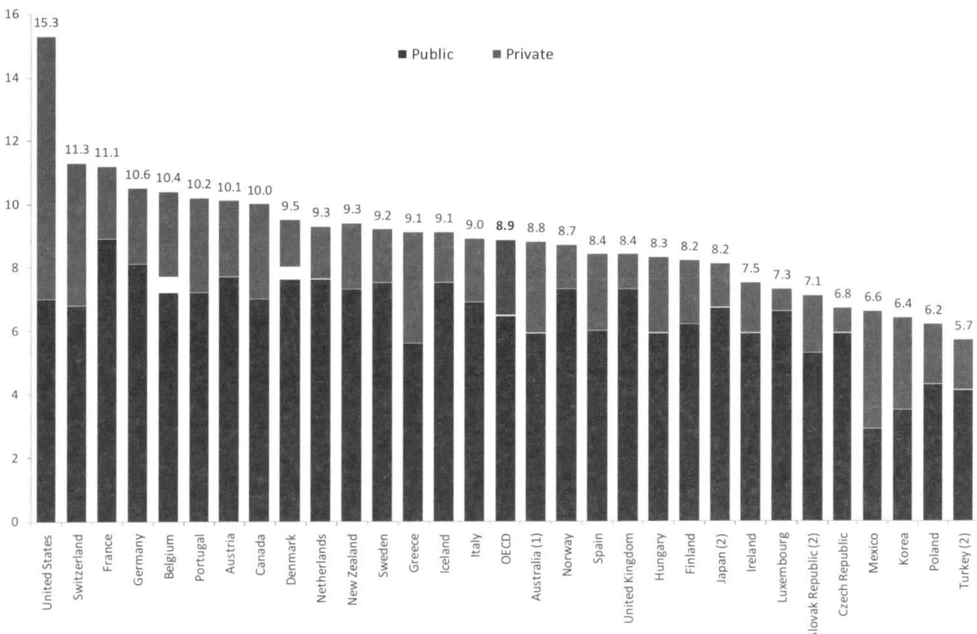

1. 2005/06.

2. 2005.

Source: OECD (2008), *OECD Health Data*.

Figure 1.6. Total health expenditure per capita (USD PPP 2000), 2006

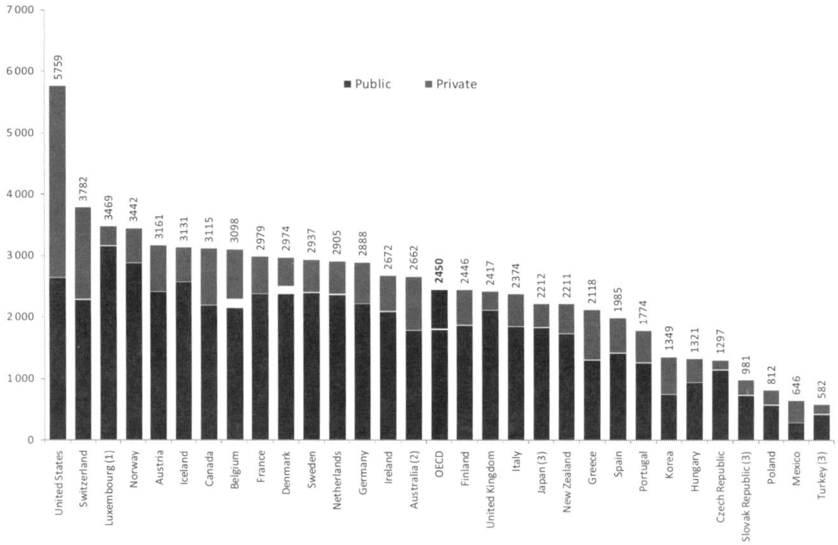

1. Covered population rather than resident population; 2. 2005/06; 3. 2005.
Source: OECD (2008), *OECD Health Data*.

Figure 1.7. Health expenditure per capita and national income per capita, 2006

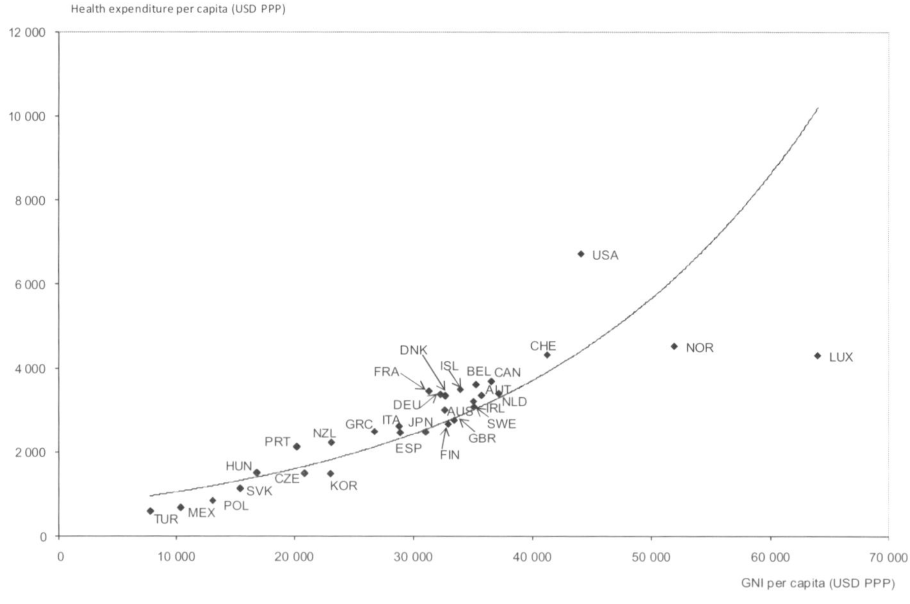

Source: OECD (2008), *OECD Health Data*.

Factors potentially contributing to differences in the level of health care spending

A large number of studies have attempted to explain cross-country differences in health care spending, often focusing on the high levels of spending in the United States.[4] Differences in income appear consistently to be an important explanatory variable, but institutional, demographic, and other variables do not fully explain the remaining variance.[5] Although the research evidence is not conclusive, policy makers still must make choices in their search for improved performance, focusing on either demand or supply-related factors, or a combination of both. The discussion below considers a number of possible reasons for cross-country differences in spending distinguishing between these two aspects. It draws on existing research and data from disparate sources. This approach is not new and was similarly used by the Congressional Research Service (2007).

Several caveats must be noted. First, the individual data items used do not always correspond neatly to the distinction made between those that represent the supply side as opposed to the demand side. For example, low use of the health care system (as measured by the number of patient contacts with primary care providers) could reflect a preference for self care or levels of cost sharing. But it may also reflect the absence of supply. For example low use of services in Mexico and Turkey may result from inadequate numbers of doctors, particularly in rural areas. As noted by Hurst and Siciliani (2004), there is a strong link between waiting lists and waiting times and spending on surgical supply.

Second, while OECD health data reflect a great effort to ensure commonality of definitions, problems of data comparability still exist. Where important difficulties remain, they are noted in the text. Finally, there remain issues of interpretation. Available data may account for some of the differences in efficiency of provision. But efficient care may not be desirable if it is ineffective in terms of health outcomes or in its technical quality.[6] Moreover, individual inputs of care cannot always be broken down into price and volume components. While data are improving, it is still difficult to identify comparable cross-country prices for medical goods such as pharmaceuticals.

Demands placed on the health system

Populations appear to vary considerably in the demands they make of the health-care system. Plausible reasons include different levels of income, the age structure of the population, the prevalence of disease, and patterns of utilisation. Differences in demand may also reflect differences in the emphasis on self-care;[7] and the presence of cost sharing or other measures limiting access to or demand for care.

Different levels of income

As has already been discussed, there is a general tendency for populations with higher income to place greater demands and spend a greater proportion of their aggregate income on health services and goods.

Age structure of the population

The composition and growth trends of a country's population can have a significant impact on health and long-term care spending both now and in future years. Since older populations tend to be in poorer health and therefore place greater demands on the health care system, it is reasonable to expect that ageing populations and the difference in demographic structure between countries may be an explanatory factor in spending differences. The percentage of the population that is 65 or above has risen and is expected to continue rising in all OECD countries. Whereas Mexico and Turkey count just a little over 5% of the population over 65, Japan, Germany, and Italy have around one person out of five above this age threshold (Figure 1.8). Indeed Figure 1.8 shows a weak but positive relationship between the share of the elderly and health spending per capita.

Patterns of disease

The prevalence of disease is also important. After circulatory disease, cancer is the second leading cause of mortality in OECD countries and the diagnosis and advanced treatment of all the various forms of cancer can account for a substantial portion of health system costs. Figure 1.9 shows the variation in age-adjusted incidence rates for all types of cancer across OECD countries and the positive relation with spending per capita. Some of this variation in incidence rates may reflect the effectiveness of the health care system in screening and, thus, diagnosing cancer.

Figure 1.8. Share of the population aged 65 and over and health spending per capita, 2006

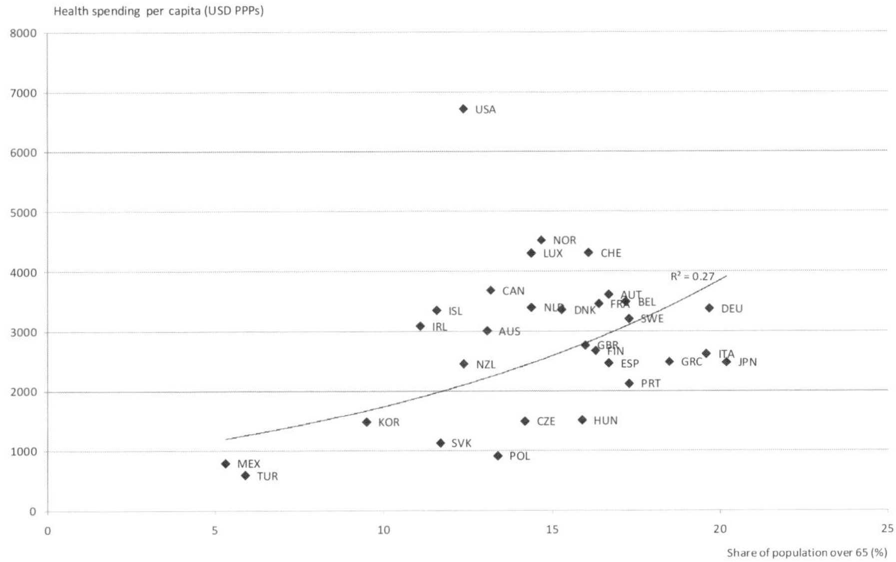

Source: OECD (2008), *OECD Health Data*.

Figure 1.9. Incidence rate for all types of cancer and health spending per capita, 2002

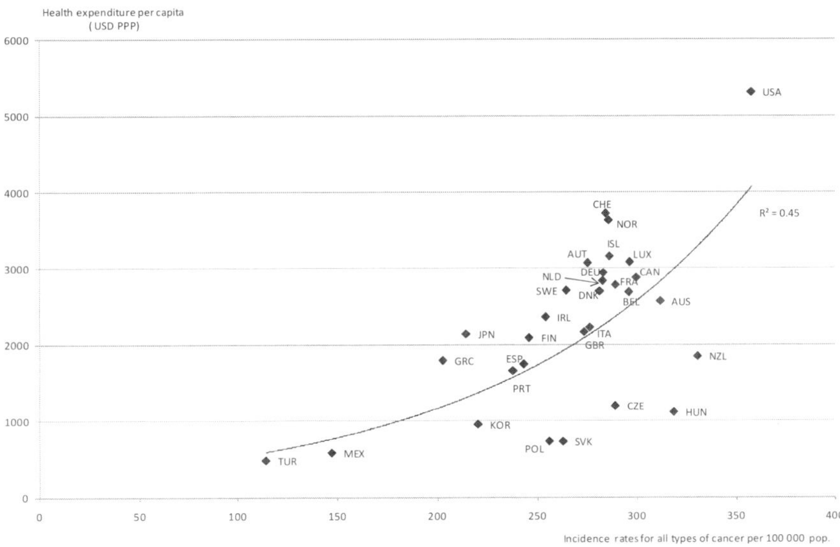

Source: OECD (2008), *OECD Health Data*.

Utilisation

The number of doctors' consultations per capita and hospital discharges can be taken as two broad indicators of in-patient and out-patient activity. Together, these two measures account for around two-thirds of health care expenditure. The data must be interpreted with caution because, as noted above, identifying the separate role of the supply side from demand remains problematic.

Although there are differences in definition and in the source of the data (administrative or survey based) across countries, variation in reported per capita consultation rates are large. There is, for example, a five-fold difference between Sweden at the lower end and Japan and the Czech Republic at the other (Figure 1.10). At the same time, some of the high-spending countries such as Canada, France, the United States, and Switzerland have levels below the OECD average.

Figure 1.10. Doctors' consultations and health spending per capita, 2005 (or latest year)

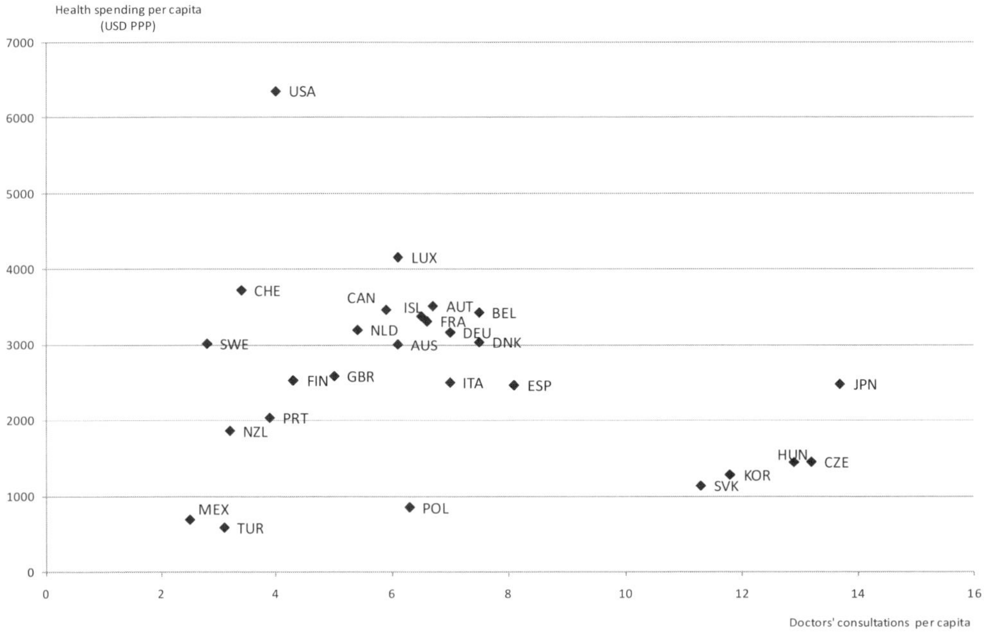

Source: OECD (2008), *OECD Health Data.*

Organisational and cultural factors may also explain variations. These include the presence of a gatekeeper system of referrals, cost-sharing arrangements, the degree and composition of specialisation, and the differing roles played by physicians relative to other health care providers.

Research suggests that systems that pay physicians based on fee for service tend to have higher consultation rates. Those with physicians paid a salary or by a system of capitation demonstrate lower rates (Fujisawa and Lafortune, 2008), suggesting that incentives associated with, provider payment methods can have an important influence on the number of services delivered.

Alternatively, differences in patient contacts may reflect the supply of providers: that is, patients see physicians less frequently in countries with lower number of physicians per capita. Figure 1.11 suggests, however, that such effects are not large, seen within this aggregate approach. Other OECD work (OECD, 2005; OECD, 2008; OECD, forthcoming) do suggest, though, that supply may be a problem in Mexico and Turkey, particularly in rural areas.

Figure 1.11. Doctors' consultations and density of physicians, 2005

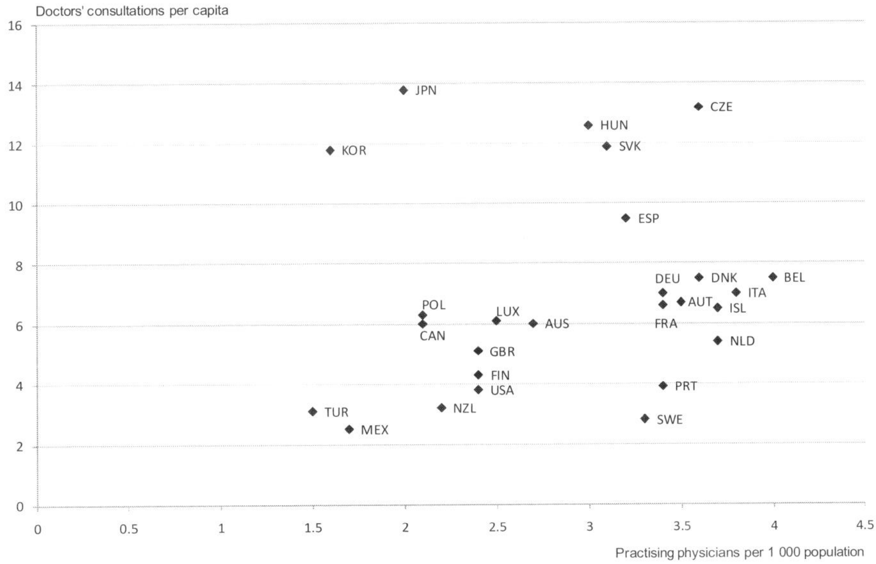

Source: OECD (2008), *OECD Health Data.*

While there is a weak association between physician supply and consultations overall, there are significant differences between countries with similar doctor densities.[8] Japan and Korea have relatively low doctor numbers but high rates of consultation. Hungary, and the Czech and Slovak Republics also show similar characteristics with relatively high doctor numbers matched by an elevated rate of doctor consultations. This may reflect cultural or organisational differences such as the time doctors spend with patients and the role doctors play in administrative tasks such as verifying sick leave or renewing prescriptions. In any case, they suggest that differences in availability of doctors do not necessarily constrain access to care. Thus, the way health care is organised may play a role in explaining cross-country differences in cost and efficiency.

Hospital discharge rates, a measure of in-patient activity, show a three-fold variation. Although differences in definition between countries can hamper international comparisons (for example, treatment of same-day admissions and transfers between units), these differences appear to reflect variation in population structure and the increased care needs of the elderly. Since the elderly account for a disproportionate percentage of overall hospital discharges (HES, 2007), countries with relatively young populations, such as Australia, Canada, Ireland, Korea and New Zealand show discharge rates below the OECD average and vice versa. (There are notable exceptions, such as Japan and Spain (Figure 1.12).[9] While some high-spending countries such as France and Germany are well above average in terms of overall discharges, others such as Switzerland and the United States are below the OECD average, once again suggesting that behaviour and institutional factors may influence these rates.

Figure 1.12. Rate of total hospital discharges and share of the population over 65, 2005

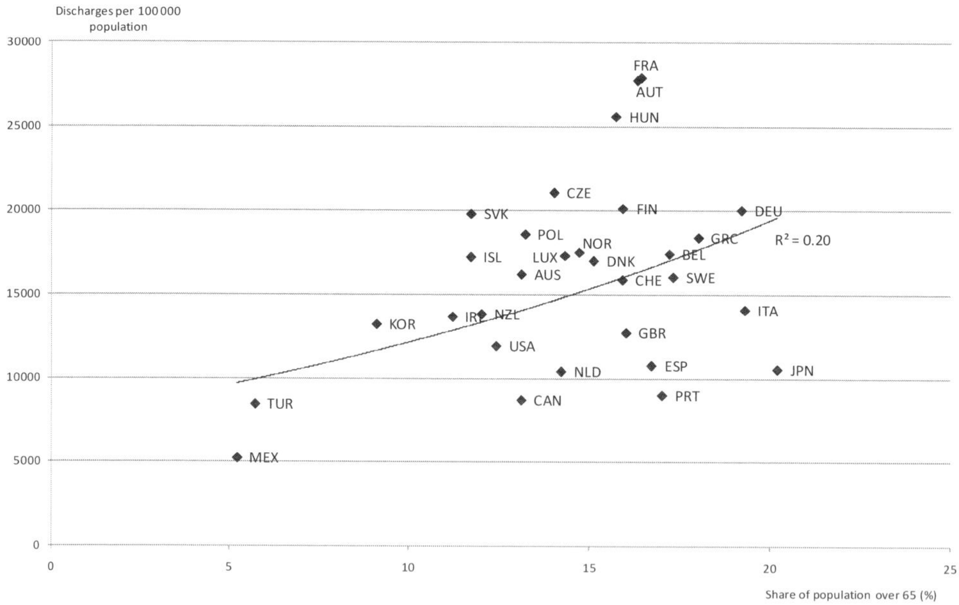

Source: OECD (2008), *OECD Health Data*.

Supply-side factors

Cross-country differences may reflect variation in the volume of inputs such as numbers of health care professionals, available physical capital such as hospital beds), and intermediate goods such as pharmaceutical drugs, and administrative costs. Such differences can also reflect the technological intensity of care.[10] Differences may also reflect variations in the prices of inputs or of the unit of care received.

Remuneration of health professionals

Variation in unit costs is potentially an important reason for cross country-differences in spending. Wages and salaries make up a large share of total health care spending and this is reflected, for example in differences in unit costs for hospital care, where hospitals are paid on the basis of a *diagnosis-related group (*DRG*)* or similar arrangements.

The remuneration of doctors [both general practitioners (GPs) and specialists] is determined in a market *where the price of physician activities is highly regulated. S*alary levels, capitation payments and fees for service are generally determined through negotiations between purchasers (for example, health ministries or health insurers) and providers (professional associations).

Available data on the remuneration of doctors and nurses suggest that unit costs of labour may differ significantly across countries. This is, of course, only a very rough measure of unit costs because total remuneration of doctors depends upon both volume and unit costs. More accurate assessment requires adjustment for hours worked.[11]

A recent OECD study using multivariate analysis examined some of the factors underlying the large variations in the remuneration of GPs and specialists across a subset of OECD countries (Fujisawa and Lafortune, 2008). While much of the variation remains unexplained, the results suggest that variations in GP remuneration are related to differences in health system characteristics (*e.g.* the methods of remuneration and the presence of a gate-keeping system) as well as supply-side factors such as the number of GPs per capita and their working hours. For specialists, fee-for-service payment (rather than salary payments), low specialist density, and longer working hours are all associated with higher remuneration levels (Figures 1.13 and 1.14).

Figure 1.13. Remuneration of general practitioners in USD PPPs, selected OECD countries, 2004 (or most recent year)

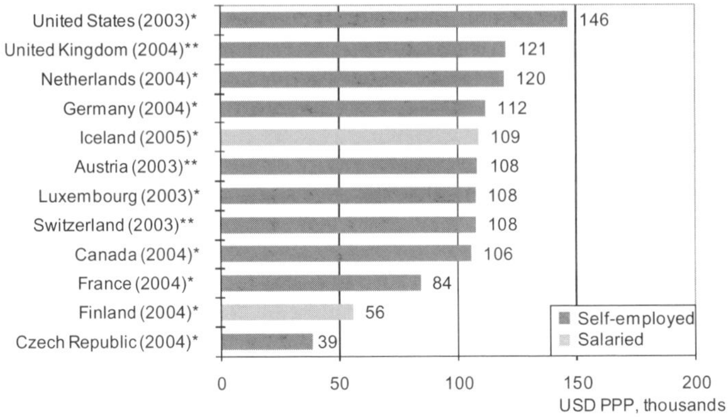

Note: *Refers only to physicians practising full-time and ** average remuneration for all physicians including those working part-time (thereby resulting in an under-estimation). In the case of Austria, Switzerland and the United States, the data refer to all physicians (both salaried and self-employed). Since most GPs are self-employed in these countries, they are presented as referring to self-employed physicians. For the United Kingdom, data refer to Great Britain.

Source: OECD (2007), *OECD Health Data*; and for the United States, HSC (2006).

Figure 1.14. Remuneration of specialists in USD PPP, selected OECD countries, 2004 (or most recent year)

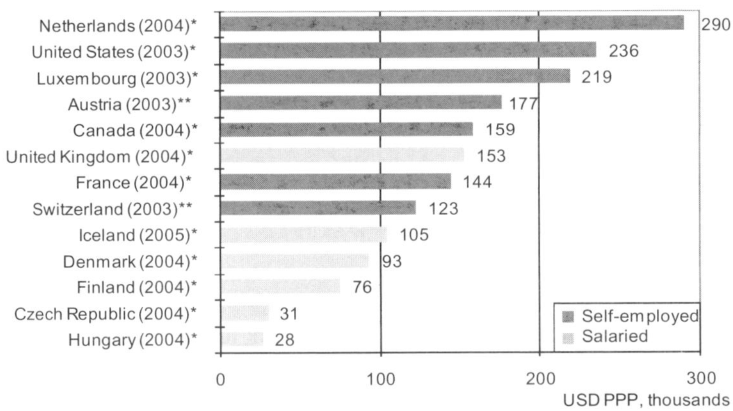

Note: PPP = Purchasing Power Parities; * refers only to physicians practising full-time and ** refers to the average remuneration for all physicians including those working part-time. In the case of Austria and Switzerland, the data refer to all physicians (both salaried and self-employed), but since most GPs are self-employed in these two countries, the data are presented as referring to self-employed physicians. For the United Kingdom, data refer to England.

Source: OECD (2007), *OECD Health Data*; and for the United States, HSC (2006),

The gap between doctors' pay and average wages widens with per capita GDP. This suggests that countries with higher average incomes may have greater difficulty in controlling wage costs in the health-care sector. This appears to be particularly the case with self-employed specialists whose incomes can be many multiples of the average national income, as is the case in the Netherlands and the United States (Figure 1.15). Further differences appear to be linked to the method of remuneration.

Figure 1.15. General practitioner and specialist remuneration as a multiple of the average national wage and gross domestic product per capita, 2004 (or most recent year)

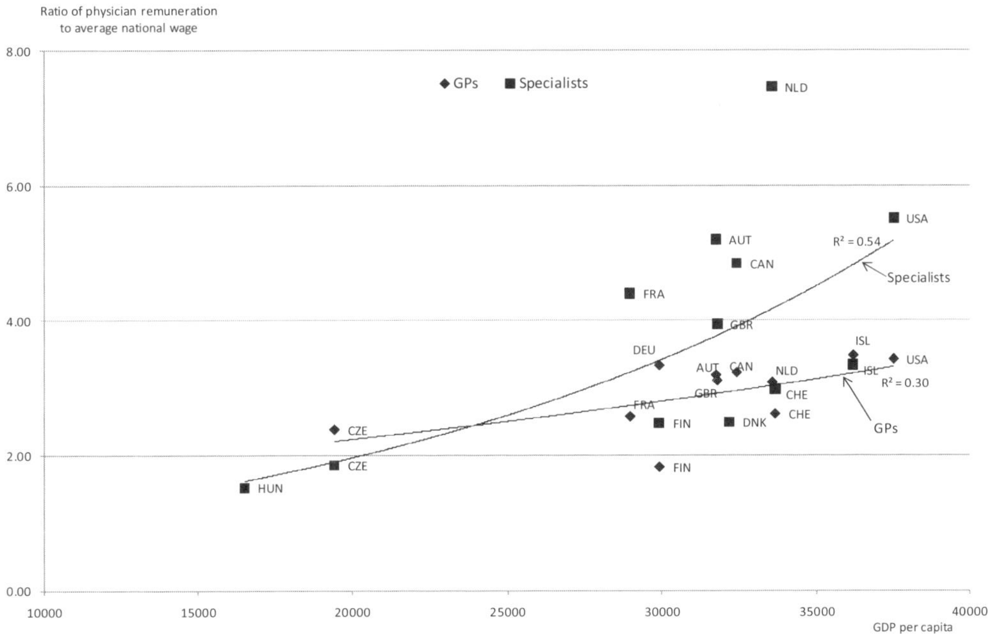

Source: OECD (2008), *OECD Health Data*.

Cross-country comparisons of nurses' salaries show less variation than for doctors, but remain, nonetheless, substantial. There is less variation across countries when nurse remunerations are normalised by per capita income (GDP). Remuneration relative to average national income (measured by per capita GDP) is highest in Portugal, followed by the United States and Australia (Figure 1.16). At the other end of the scale, nurses' salaries are lower than the national income in the Czech Republic, Hungary, and Norway.

Figure 1.16. Remuneration for nurses: ratio with relation to GDP per capita, 2005

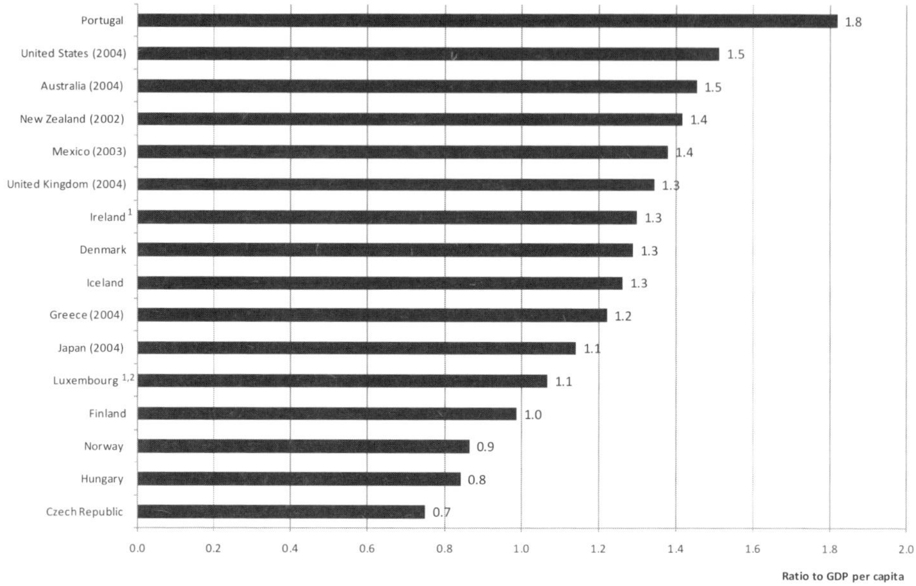

1. Given that GDP per capita overstates the average income, remuneration is presented as a ratio to the gross national income.

2. Luxembourg includes nursing aides.

Source: OECD (2008), *OECD Health Data*.

Unit costs in hospitals

Ready-made data on hospital unit costs that permit comprehensive international comparisons are not yet available (Häkkinen and Joumard, 2007). Nonetheless, an exploratory study in ten OECD countries of hospital unit costs (as proxied by DRGs) for seven pathologies suggests significant cross-country differences in unit costs (Erlandsen, 2007). This work suggests that, on average, if unit costs were reduced to the level of the best performers, average costs could potentially be reduced by 5% and 48% (Figure 1.17). In addition, preliminary results from a four-country comparison of Nordic hospitals show that hospital efficiency varies considerably, even between countries with relatively similar institutional features, with cost-saving potential ranging on average from 23% to 44% (Kittelsen *et al.*, 2007). The evidence on within-country dispersion also indicates large cross-country differences. To the extent that higher dispersion indicates a potential for efficiency gains, there could be substantial scope for improvements within several countries by bringing the performance of inefficient hospitals up to best national practice.

Figure 1.17. Potential for reduction in unit costs across countries for seven hospital interventions, 2006

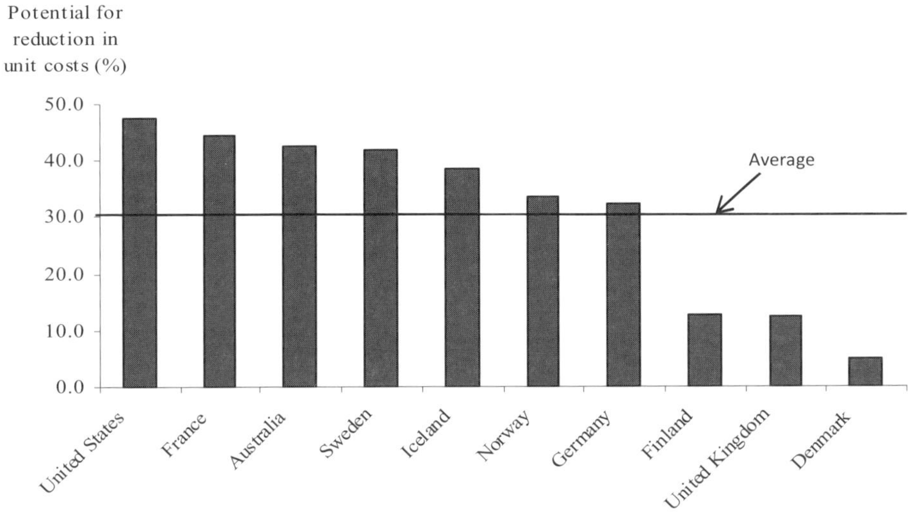

Source: Erlandsen, E. (2007), "Improving the Efficiency of Health Care Spending: Selected Evidence on Hospital Performance", OECD Economic Department Working Paper No. 555, OECD Publishing, Paris.

Differences in the supply of health professionals

The number of physicians and nurses has grown significantly over the past 30 years in all OECD countries. In itself, this leads to higher expenditure. To the extent that doctors can induce demand for care or there is pent-up demand, the effects may be even greater. Whatever the relationship between cause and effect, the indirect costs of doctors' diagnostic and treatment decisions appear to have grown steadily in most OECD countries. On average, health expenditure per physician has increased around one-third in real terms between 1990 and 2005. Rising physician numbers, increased specialisations and higher spending by physicians may also lead to improvements in the technical quality of care for selected conditions in some countries (OECD, 2007).

Looking across countries, there is evidence of a positive link between income (as measured by GDP) and the density of health care workers, particularly physicians, which may partly explain the positive relation between spending and per capita income shown in Figure 1.7. There is, however, little relation between the level of GDP per capita or remuneration levels of physicians and the density of physicians. Many other factors, including controls on medical school intake, regulation, and regional characteristics, are at work. Thus, despite high levels of spending per capita and a large share of spending in GDP, the United States and Canada both have physician numbers below the OECD average (Figure 1.18).

Figure 1.18. Practising physicians per 1 000 population, 2006

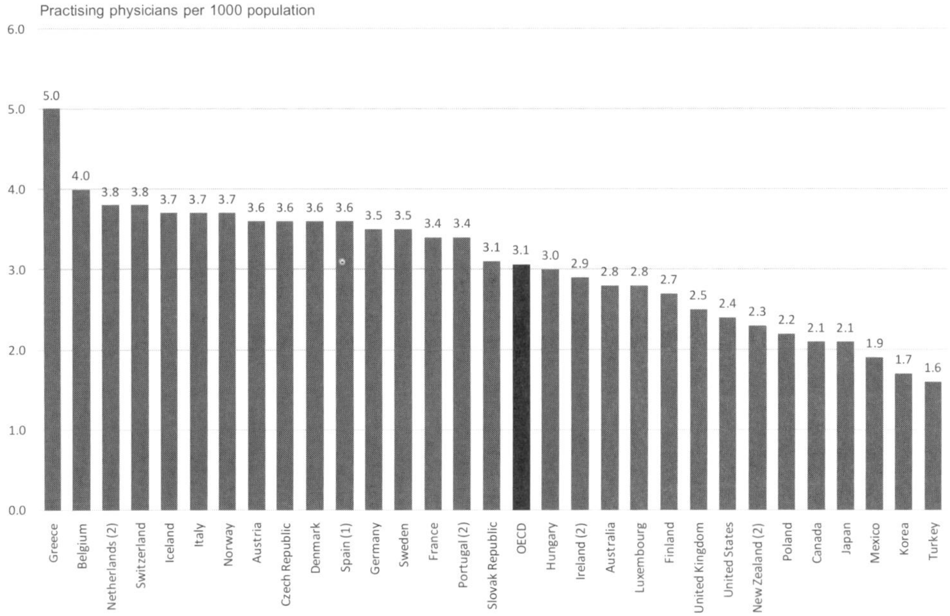

1. Includes dentists and stomatologists.

2. Physicians entitled to practise rather than practising.

Source: OECD (2008), *OECD Health Data*.

In 2005, there were also considerable cross-country differences in nurse supply, ranging from less than 2 per 1 000 population in Korea and Turkey to more than 15 in Norway and Ireland although this may not accurately reflect skill levels.[12] To adjust for different average lengths of hospital stay (ALOS) in OECD countries, Figure 1.19 presents the number of nurses expressed per bed-day (Angrisano, 2007). Countries such as Spain and the United States with relatively low nurse densities but low ALOS feature higher numbers; the contrary is true in the Czech Republic and Japan.

Figure 1.19. Practising nurses per 1 000 bed-days, 2005

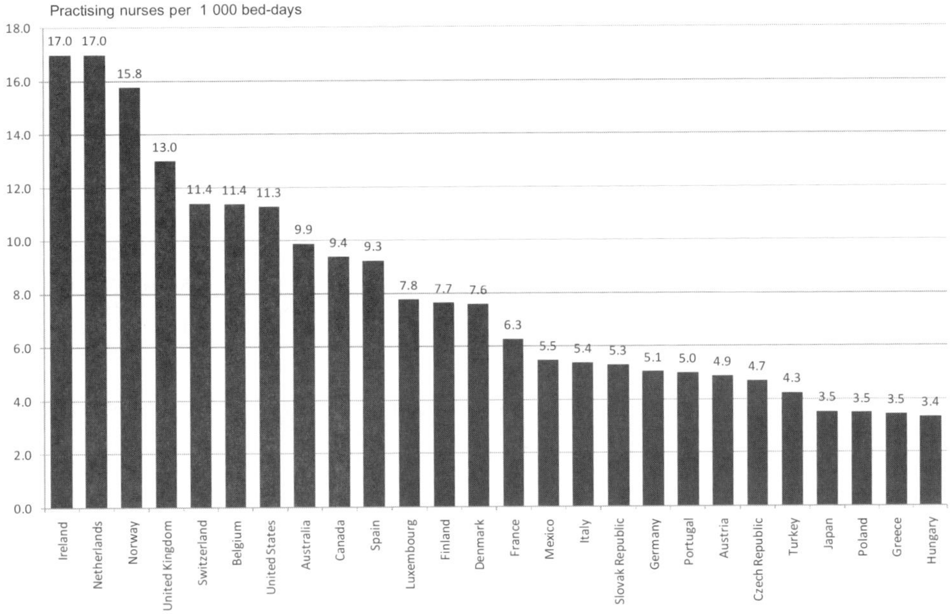

Note: Number of nurses includes those working outside of the hospital sector.

Source: OECD (2007), *OECD Health Data*.

On the one hand, less invasive techniques and reductions in average lengths of stay and acute care beds can exert downward pressure on nurse numbers. On the other, increases in skills and the need for more care of a chronic long-term nature (especially for the elderly) can increase demand for nurses.

Levels of acute care beds and average length of stay

Most OECD countries have seen falling bed numbers and shorter average length of stay over recent decades. Length of stay is one important dimension in assessing efficiency: the shorter the length of stay, the lower the cost for any given treatment. However, such measures also need to take into account the intensity of the services provided (*e.g.* use of high-tech imaging or high-cost cancer treatments) and case mix. Finally, any implications for efficiency need to take account of the risk of poorer health outcomes or readmission in the case of premature discharge from the hospital.

The number of acute beds varies significantly across OECD countries, ranging from over six acute care beds per 1 000 population in Australia, Germany, Japan and Korea to around just over two or less in Mexico, Sweden and Turkey. The average length of stay shows a positive relationship with the available bed numbers (Figure 1.20) although this relationship has become progressively weaker over time (Oxley and Macfarlan, 1995). Higher capacity can lead to increased length of stay, particularly where hospitals are paid for on a bed-day basis or where acute-care beds are being used for long-term care. High ALOS rates are observed in Japan, Korea, and Germany where payment has, until recently, largely been on the basis of bed days. Low ALOS rates were reported in some of the Nordic countries and Mexico. The use of DRG prospective payment systems may encourage shorter stays.

Figure 1.20. Acute care hospital beds and average length of stay in hospitals, 2005

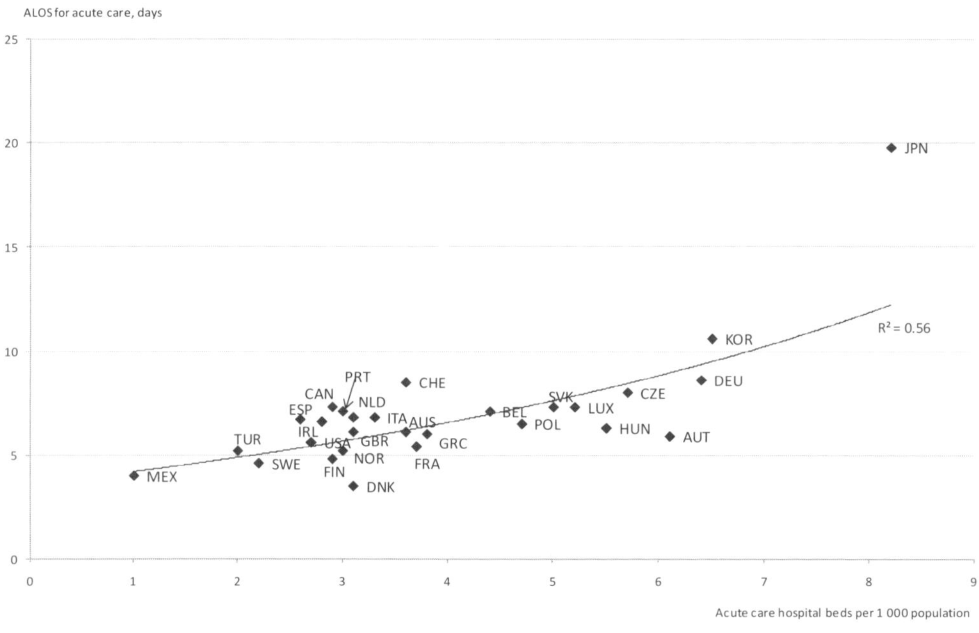

Source: OECD (2007), *OECD Health Data*.

Intensity of care and the use of technology

In examining differences in hospital expenditures, it is also important to consider the intensity of the care received and the volume of high cost medical care. For example, data on the number of cardio-vascular procedures performed show the United States at twice the OECD average (Figure 1.21). By contrast, the rate in Switzerland is less than half the OECD average. *The* introduction of expensive medical technology *does not always increase* discharge rates. *For example, same-day surgery for cataracts resulted in a* shift away from hospital in-patient *admissions. And* increased use of pharmaceuticals has permitted certain chronically ill individuals to be hospitalised less frequently.

Figure 1.21. Coronary revascularisation procedures, per 100 000 population, 2004

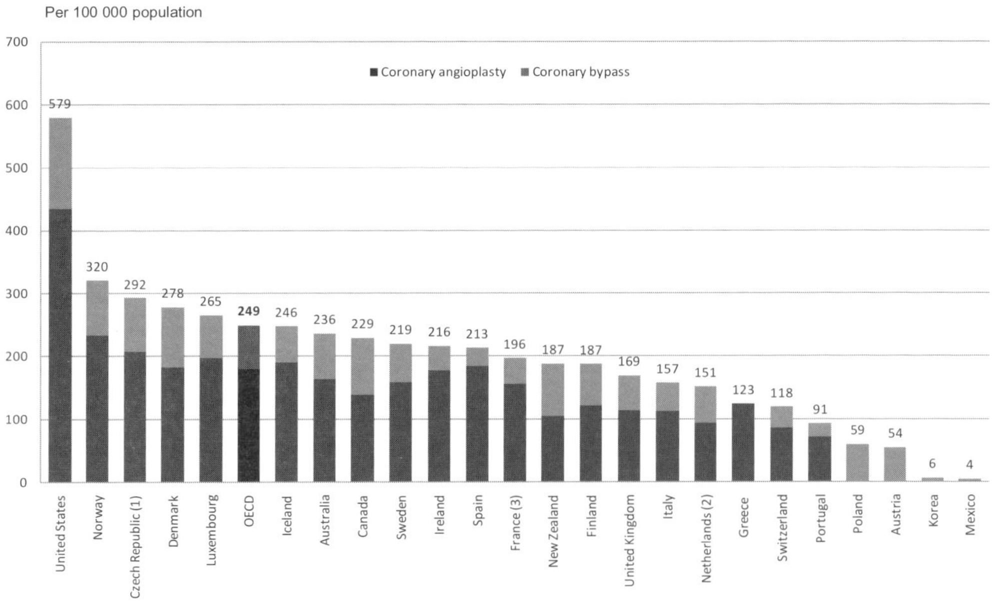

Source: OECD (2007), *OECD Health Data*.

The diffusion of medical technology is also seen as one of the drivers of health spending across the OECD. The number of magnetic resonance imaging (MRI) machines per 1 million population (Figure 1.22) is one marker of the supply of technology, although these numbers do not indicate the extent to which equipment is actually used. Figures for the United States actually under-estimate availability since data refer to the number of hospitals rather than the number of machines. Health spending per capita is positively correlated with the diffusion of such technologies, controlling for a number of possible explanatory factors (Eun-Hwan Oh *et al.*, 2005).

Figure 1.22. Per capita spending on curative care and number of MRI machines, 2006

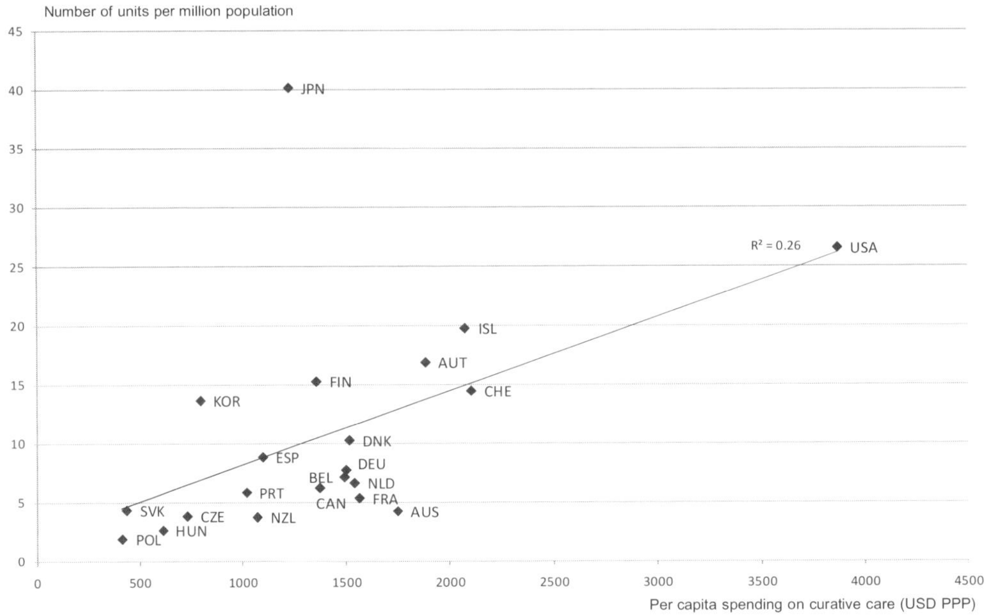

Source: OECD (2008), *OECD Health Data*.

Expenditure for pharmaceuticals

As mentioned above, spending on pharmaceuticals has grown significantly. Population ageing and the diffusion of new drugs have pushed up consumption and costs over recent years. The effect on overall spending, however, is not simple since the introduction of drugs to tackle certain diseases or conditions may reduce the need for costly hospitalisation or surgical interventions.

Figure 1.23. Pharmaceutical expenditure per capita (USD PPP 2000) and share of gross domestic product, 2006

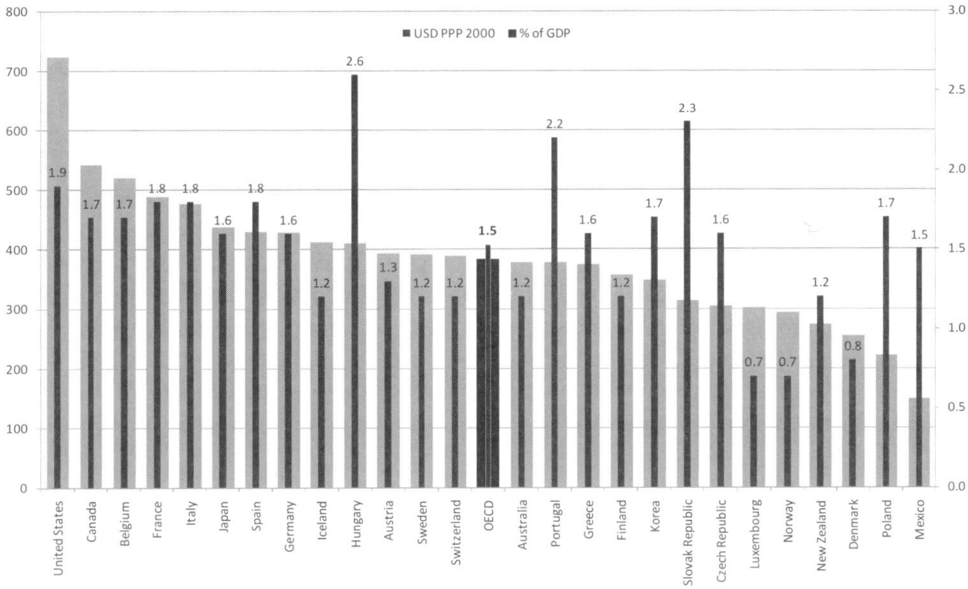

1. Prescription medicines only.

2. 2004. 3. 2004/05.

Source: OECD (2008), *OECD Health Data*.

Figure 1.23 shows the average per capita spending on pharmaceuticals with the United States the highest spender with almost USD 800 per capita, almost twice the OECD average. Aside from Mexico, Poland, Denmark, and New Zealand were the lowest spenders. Pharmaceutical spending accounted for 1.5% of GDP, and ranged between 0.8% in Ireland, Norway, and Denmark up to 2.2-2.4% in Portugal, the Slovak Republic, and Hungary. Per capita pharmaceutical spending varies much less than health spending overall. The differences in pharmaceutical spending reflect the differences in consumption patterns, the quantities of pharmaceuticals consumed, and the difference in prices between countries.

Administrative costs

Examining spending on administration provides further hints on the source of differences in health-care spending. Figure 1.24 shows the share of current health spending devoted to health administration and insurance. Highly fragmented and complex multi-payer health systems may require more overall administration than single payer systems. Countries with health systems based primarily on health insurance schemes – either public, private or both – appear to report a much higher share of spending on administration when compared to those with tax-funded national health services. However, these results should not be taken at face value. Because it is often difficult for countries to fully allocate administrative costs of all ministries involved in the planning, co-ordination, budgeting and provision of health services, costs may be underestimated. In the same vein, it is often difficult for private insurance companies to distinguish administrative expenditure related to health insurance from the other types of insurance they may offer. Finally, the administrative spending reported here refers only to centrally based planning and management activities and not to the administrative activities of primary and secondary health providers, where complex multi-payer systems may also have an impact on the resource costs of their administrative systems and on the overall costs of health insurance.[13]

Figure 1.24. Spending on health administration and health insurance as a share of current health expenditure, 2006

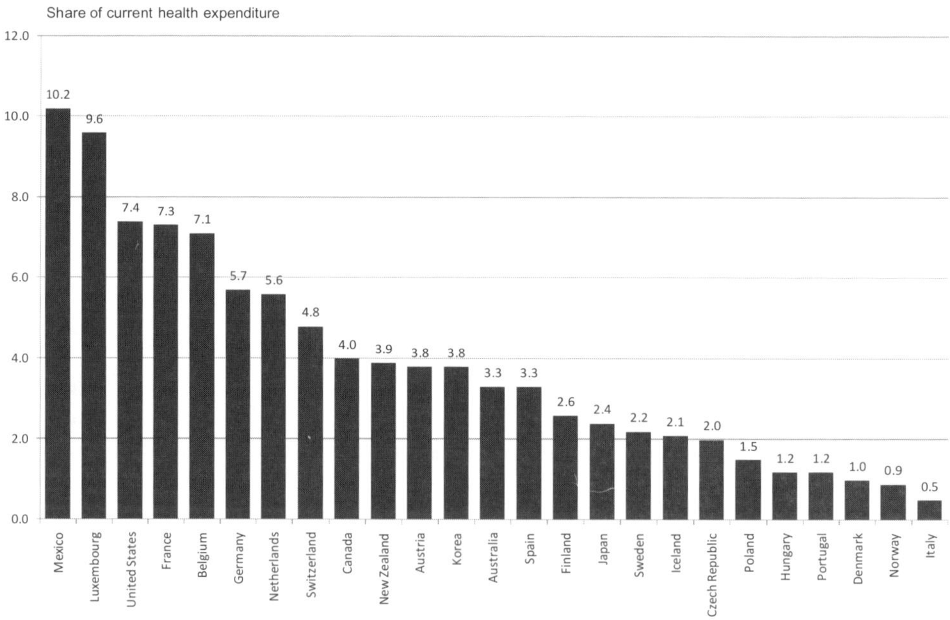

Source: OECD (2008), *OECD Health Data*.

Differences in health care spending: the broader picture

Expenditure patterns differ substantially across OECD countries in terms of prices, volume, and type of service. While it is difficult to make definitive statements about the reasons for these differences, they are summarised in Table 1.1 by arraying countries by their quartile ranking for various indicators such as demand for care, price, volume and expenditure on pharmaceutical drugs and administration. The factors included were selected based on available data and are not exhaustive. Additional research would be needed in order to examine the suitability of each indicator in explaining expenditure variation. While these do not provide clear answers as to reasons for the level of spending in individual countries, it can, nonetheless, provide a check list of potential areas of success and of concern.

Table 1.1. Summary of factors potentially contributing to differences in health spending across countries

	Share of population over 65	GNI per capita	Cancer incidence	Remuneration GPs	Remuneration specialists	Remuneration nurses	Number of physicians	Nurses per bedday	Acute care beds	MRI machines	Coronary Angioplasty	Coronary Bypass	Pharmaceutical spending	Administrative costs	Share of GDP on health
2006 or latest data															
Australia	↘	↘	↑	↓	↑	↑	↘	↗	↗	↘	↗	↗	↗	↗	↗
Austria	↗	↗	↘	↗	↑		↗	↓	↑	↑		↘	↗	↗	↗
Belgium	↑	↗	↑	↘	↑	↑	↑	↗	↑	↗	↑	↑		↑	↑
Canada	↘	↑	↑	↗	↗		↓	↗	↘	↘	↘	↑	↑	↗	↗
Czech Republic	↘	↓	↗	↓	↓	↓	↗	↓	↑	↓	↗	↗	↘	↘	↓
Denmark	↘	↑	↘		↘	↗	↗	↘	↗	↗	↗	↗	↓	↘	↗
Finland	↗	↗	↓	↓	↓	↓	↘	↗	↗	↑	↘	↘	↘	↓	↓
France	↗	↘	↗	↘	↑		↗	↘	↗	↘			↑	↑	↑
Germany	↑	↘	↗	↑	↘		↗	↘	↑	↗	↑	↗	↑	↑	↑
Greece	↑	↓	↓		↓	↘	↑	↓	↗	↗	↘		↗		↘
Hungary	↗	↓	↑	↓	↓	↓	↘	↓	↑	↓	↑	↑	↘	↓	↓
Iceland	↓	↘	↗	↘	↘	↗	↑			↑	↗	↓	↑	↘	↘
Ireland	↓	↗	↓	↑	↗	↘	↘	↑	↘		↓	↓	↓		↓
Japan	↑	↘	↓	↘		↘	↓	↓	↑	↑			↑	↘	↓
Mexico	↓	↓	↓	↗	↗	↑	↓	↘	↓	↓	↓	↓	↓	↘	↓
Netherlands	↘	↑	↘	↑	↑		↑	↑	↗	↘	↓	↘	↓	↗	↗
New Zealand	↓	↓	↑		↗	↑	↓			↓	↓	↗	↓	↗	↗
Norway	↘	↑	↗		↓	↓	↑	↑	↘		↑	↑	↘	↓	↘
Portugal	↑	↓	↓		↘	↑	↗	↘	↘	↓	↓	↓	↗	↓	↑
Sweden	↑	↗	↘	↓	↓		↗		↓		↗	↘	↓	↓	↘
Switzerland	↗	↑	↗	↗	↘		↑	↑	↗	↗	↘	↓	↗	↑	↑
United Kingdom	↗	↗	↘	↑	↗	↗	↘	↑	↓	↘	↘	↘	↘		↘
United States	↓	↑	↑	↑	↑	↑	↘	↗	↓	↑	↑	↑	↑	↑	↑

GNI: Gross national income.

In this procedure, the median country is identified for each indicator and countries are separated into those lying above and below the median country. The indicators are then broken down further into the four quartiles. Depending on the grouping, countries are described using the following identifiers ⇩ for countries in the bottom quartile; ⬂ for countries in the third quartile; ⬀ for countries lying in the second quartile and ⇧ for countries in the top quartile. Note that data for some countries are not available in some dimensions. The same procedure has been used in the right hand column for spending as a share of GDP in the latest available year for each country.

One could argue that the wider the variance among countries, the greater the scope for improving efficiency-related performance of health care systems. That is, performance could be improved by bringing individual observations closer to the mean. But this is too simplistic. As shown in Table 1.1 some countries lie above the median in some dimensions and below the median in others and there may be cases of trade-off between them. For example, a deeper analysis of Table 1.1 suggests that countries with high remuneration and unit costs relative to the median country also tend to be those with lower levels of inputs and vice versa. Such patterns may reflect specific policy choices concerning the balance between efficiency and other goals. It may also reflect the institutional relationships and policies peculiar to individual countries that govern health care demand and supply. Moreover, not all of the possible dimensions have been highlighted and some of these may be of greater importance for some countries than in others. More work needs to be done to identify better the underlying linkages between individual indicators and spending patterns.

Conclusions

This chapter draws on existing information on health system spending to highlight the wide variance across countries in levels of spending and growth in spending. Several questions arise after examining these data. First, it is important to assess whether the recent slowdown in expenditure growth is a beginning of a new trend or a short hiatus in the otherwise upward trend in spending as a share of GDP over recent decades. The examination of the recent past suggests that continued vigilance is required. In this context, policy makers would certainly benefit from a further analysis of which countries have experienced the sharpest deceleration in spending in the most recent period, the extent to which this is the result of specific policies, and the prospects for long-term sustainability.

Second, despite more rapid growth in spending on pharmaceuticals, the hospital sector remains the largest contributor to over-all spending growth. The share of spending going to hospital and ambulatory care in many countries has been relatively stable despite the growing need to shift resources to an outpatient or an ambulatory environment as chronic disease increases with population ageing.

Turning to the variation across-countries in spending patterns, there are a number of hypotheses concerning the source of differences in spending. This work is exploratory and needs further development. While accepting the caveats expressed previously, one cannot be but struck by the variation across countries in many of the indicators and by the need to understand why this should be so. These differences are very marked for demand-related variables and understanding the reasons for this is of particular interest for policy makers. On the supply side, a number of indicators suggest that outcomes are a reflection of the institutional features and ways of paying providers. As stressed in earlier work from the OECD (OECD, 2004), policy makers will need to pay close attention to the incentives built into their health care systems.

Notes

1. Depending on the scenario, the share of health and long-term care expenditures in GDP could increase by between 3.5 to more than 6 percentage points of GDP on average across OECD countries between 2005 and 2050 (Oliveira Martens and de la Maisonneuve, 2006).

2. For example, policies to limit the growth in the remuneration of health care providers or the supply of health services are likely to be followed by a rise as markets reassert themselves (as occurred in Canada and England from the beginning of this decade). When waiting lists develop for certain services, political pressure often builds up to reduce them (Docteur and Oxley, 2004; Siciliani and Hurst, 2004).

3. It is worth noting that the average share of spending going to ambulatory and hospital care respectively has remained broadly unchanged over the past decade, despite the abovementioned rise in ambulatory spending in some countries and the need to improve ambulatory care for the growing numbers of the chronically ill (Hofmarcher *et al.*, 2007).

4. See Oxley and Macfarlan (1994); Gerdham and Jönsson (2000); Congressional Research Service (2007); and McKinsey Global Institute (2007).

5. Gerdham and Jönsson (2000) found that gatekeeping systems and the payment methods, particularly for primary care, explaining some of the cross-country differences.

6. For example, as shown by Joumard *et al.* (2008), there can be important differences in indicators of health outcomes across countries after levels of inputs have been controlled for.

7. For example there are marked differences in Switzerland between the demand for health care between the French speaking and German speaking cantons).

8. See, for example, countries grouped between two and three, and three and four doctors per 10 000.

9. Data from Japan are not easily comparable with other countries due to the high level of beds used for long-term care. The actual number of acute-care discharges may be lower.

10. For example the high level of coronary revascularisation in the United States is shown below.

11. More precise measures of doctor activities that go beyond working time – such as the volume and types of services provided – could be useful additional explanatory variables were they available. More information on amounts paid to doctors for different types of services is also needed to understand more fully variations in remuneration and to decompose price and volume effects. The analysis has been hampered by incomparability of available data on the remuneration of doctors. High rates for the United States may also reflect the fact that medical schools are fee paying and receive little public support.

12. For example, Ireland may include nurse assistants (OECD, 2008).

13. Consideration may also need to be given to what is contained in (or obtained from) administrative costs. For example, higher administrative costs in insurance based systems may also reflect attempts to assess the quality of care of individual providers.

Bibliography

Angrisano, C., et al. (2007), *Accounting for the Cost of Health Care in the United States*, McKinsey & Company, San Francisco.

Center for Studying Health System Change (HSC) (2006), "Losing Ground: Physician Income, 1995-2003", Tracking Report No. 15, HSC, Washington, DC.

Colombo, F. and D. Morgan (2006), "Evolution of Health Expenditure in OECD Countries", *Revue Française des Affaires Sociales*, April-September.

Docteur, E. and H. Oxley (2004), "Health System Reform: Lessons from Experience", in OECD (2004), *Towards High Performing Health Systems: Policy Studies,* OECD Publishing, Paris.

Erlandsen, E. (2007), "Improving the Efficiency of Health Care Spending: Selected Evidence on Hospital Performance", OECD Economic Department Working Paper No. 555, OECD Publishing, Paris.

Eun-Hwan Oh, Y. Imanaka and E. Evans (2005), "Determinants of the Diffusion of Computed Tomography and Magnetic Resonance Imaging", *International Journal of Technology Assessment in Health Care*, Vol. 21, No. 1, pp. 73-80.

Fujisawa, R. and G. Lafortune (2008), "The Remuneration of General Practitioners and Specialists in 14 OECD Countries: What are the Factors Influencing Variations Across Countries?", OECD Health Working Paper, No. 34, OECD Publishing, Paris.

Häkkinen, U. and I. Joumard (2007), "Cross-CountryAnalysis of Efficiency in OECD Health Care Sectors: Options for Research", OECD Economics Department Working Paper No. 554, OECD Publishing, Paris.

Gerdham, U. and B. Jönsson (2000), "International Comparisons of Health Expenditure: Theory, Data and Econometric Analysis", in A. Cuyler and J. Newhouse (eds.), *Handbook of Health Economics*, Elsevier, Amsterdam.

HES (2007), *Hospital Episode Statistics, Headline Figures, 2006-07,* The Information Centre, United Kingdom. Available at *www.hesonline.nhs.uk.*

Hurst, J. and L. Siciliani (2004), "Tackling Excessive Waiting Times for Elective Surgery", in OECD (2004), *Towards High Performing Health Systems: Policy Studies,* OECD Publishing, Paris.

Joumard, I. *et al.* (2008), "Health Status Determinants: Lifestyle, Environment, Health Care Resources and Efficiency", OECD Economics Department Working Paper, No. 627, OECD Publishing, Paris.

Kittelsen, S.A.C., J. Magnussen and K.S. Anthun (2007), "Sykehus-produktivitet etter statlig overtakelse: En nordisk komparativ analyse" (Hospital productivity after transfer of ownership from local to central government – a Nordic comparative analysis), *HERO Skriftserie 2007:1*, University of Oslo, Norway.

McKinsey Global Institute (2007), *Accounting for the Cost of Health Care in the United States,* Washington, DC.

OECD (2004), *Towards High Performing Health Systems*, OECD Publishing, Paris.

OECD (2005), *OECD Reviews of Health Systems: Mexico*, OECD Publishing, Paris.

OECD (2007a), *OECD Health Data* 2007, OECD Publishing, Paris.

OECD (2007b), *Health at a Glance 2007 – OECD Indicators*, OECD Publishing, Paris.

OECD (2008), *OECD Health Data 2008*, OECD Publishing, Paris.

Oliveira Martens, M. J. and C. de la Maisonneuve (2006), "The Drivers of Public Expenditure on Health and Long-Term Care: An Integrated Approach", *OECD Economic Studies*, No. 42, OECD Publishing, Paris.

Oxley, H. and M. Macfarlan (1994), "Health Care Reform Controlling Spending and Increasing Efficiency", OECD Economics Department Working Papers No. 149, OECD Publishing, Paris.

Peterson, C. and R. Burton (2007), *U.S. Health Care Spending: Comparisons with other OECD Countries,* Congressional Research Service, Order Code No. RL34175, September 17, Washington, DC.

Chapter 2.

Market Mechanisms and the Use of Health Care Resources

By Peter C. Smith,
Professor of Health Policy, Imperial College Business School, London

This chapter examines the potential role of competition and markets in the health sector, describes experience to date, and seeks to draw out the important policy issues for the future.

Introduction

Ever since Adam Smith developed the concept of the invisible hand, many people have assumed that the discipline of economics is synonymous with the study of competition and markets, and that economists promote the notion of competition as the principal mechanism for improving social welfare.[1] Certainly the behaviour of buyers and sellers is a major topic of study amongst economists. However, only a few zealots now adhere absolutely to the belief that competition offers an unalloyed solution to society's more intractable problems. Even the most elementary course in conventional economics tells us that markets unambiguously confer benefits on society only in the most special circumstances – where there are large numbers of buyers and sellers, where information is freely available to all, where there are no transaction costs, where property rights can be enforced, and so on. Once we depart from such circumstances, the virtues of the market become much less obvious, and society may need to implement measures (such as market regulation) to correct market failures, in the extreme perhaps abandoning market exchange for some other method of allocating society's resources.

In no sector of the economy can the departure from the neoclassical economist's assumptions underlying a competitive market be more pronounced than in the field of health care (Smith, 2000). To name but a few of the violations:

- Consumers (patients) are relatively uninformed about the characteristics of the health care on offer;
- There are other major information gaps throughout the health system, especially concerning the clinical outcomes achieved;
- Providers (and in particular physicians) play a key role in influencing the health care demanded and received by the patient;
- In many specialties and geographic locations there exists little realistic choice of provider;
- Exit and entry to health care markets is severely circumscribed by practical and regulatory constraints;
- Patients rarely bear directly the full cost of health care received;
- Many aspects of health care, such as research and development, and education and training, have the characteristics of a public good, which traditional markets cannot deliver on their own ;

- Society frequently has objectives relating to equity and solidarity that may conflict with the efficiency criteria underlying a pure market approach.

At the same time, sole reliance on non-market mechanisms, such as the public sector, also gives rise to serious problems. Health services are a uniquely complex sector of the economy. There are unclear lines of accountability, between patients, providers, governments, taxpayers, and provider institutions such as hospitals that offer enormous opportunities for opportunistic behaviour and inefficiency. Promoting rational use of resources in any health system is therefore a challenging undertaking in which governments also fail.

As a result, and notwithstanding the profound obstacles to securing an efficient market in health care, many developed nations are seeking to introduce market-type mechanisms into their health care systems. Attention is increasingly turning towards examining the circumstances in which market instruments can enhance innovation, productivity, and performance, and what additional instruments may be needed in order to assure improvements in line with society's objectives.

This chapter examines the potential role of competition and markets in the health sector, describes experience to date, and seeks to draw out the important policy issues for the future. It begins by examining the research evidence from experience with markets and competition to date. It then looks at three types of competition that give rise to quite different sets of provider incentives: competition for health insurance, for collectively purchased health services, and for individual patients. The third section considers how current policies might be improved, and the final section draws some conclusions.

Experience to date

The market has historically been the dominant mechanism for delivering health care, and remains so in much of the developing world. It is only in the last 100 years, and particularly in the last 50 years, that social health insurance has become ubiquitous in the developed world, tempering the traditional market with other regulatory and governance structures. Moreover, this chapter is concerned with market-type mechanisms rather than markets per se. Numerous aspects of health system architecture can provide elements of market-type competition, without necessarily resorting to markets in the conventional sense. Indeed, I shall focus primarily on competition as the more fundamental spur to health system improvement, and not solely on markets. This section examines experience to date. It draws mainly on published research literature, and therefore is quite selective in the examples it gives. However, this enables me to comment wherever possible on the effectiveness of policies.

Broadly speaking, three types of competition in health care can be identified: competition for the insurance function, competition for collectively purchased health services, and competition for individual treatments. These types of competition often interact. For example, in some social health insurance systems, increased competition in the insurance market is seen as one means of enhancing efficiency through greater competition amongst providers.

Competition for health care insurance

Competition for the insurance function has long been a feature of the health care system in the United States, and has increasingly become a major development in some social insurance health systems (Colombo and Tapay, 2004). In essence, for each person, there is competition to provide insurance for specified health services for a specified period such as a year. The relevant health services could be specified generally (all necessary health care within a general health basket) or quite narrowly (primary care services), and could be applied to people in general, or to patients with an established condition (such as end stage renal failure). In order for competition to operate properly, there must be an opportunity for insurees periodically (typically once a year) to review their insurance provider, and to decide whether or not to re-enrol.

Central to the insurance market is the payment mechanism adopted. In any insurance market, the expected health care costs of each potential insuree must be accurately assessed. In an unregulated voluntary insurance market, where the payer is the individual, insurers assess the expenditure risks associated with his or her circumstances, and offer an associated premium and benefit package. The major body of experience in this domain is from the United States, where many persons below the age of 65 (or their employers) seek out an insurance package in line with their preferences from a range of competitors (OECD Health Project, 2004). In practice, the choices of many Americans is seriously circumscribed, either because they are locked into particular plans through their employment, or because they lack the means to insure, or because insurers are able to decline those they perceive to be bad risks (Smith *et al.*, 2005).

Of more interest from a policy perspective are the policy experiments with competition in social health insurance in countries such as the Belgium, Germany, Israel, the Netherlands, and Switzerland (van de Ven *et al.*, 2003, 2007). While the precise elements of these systems vary, insurance is mandatory and competing insurers must accept any applicant on the basis of a community rated premium for a statutory package of care that all insurers must offer. They must also allow periodic re-enrolment, when individuals are permitted to change insurer. The criteria for a person's choice of insurer might include the scope of the offered package, the perceived quality of care, the size of any supplementary premiums (for coverage of additional risks not included in the statutory package), and any side benefits offered by the insurer. The intention is to stimulate insurers to become more administratively efficient, provide better services to their clients and, to eventually search for more efficient and better quality providers and seek out cost-effective technological innovations. However, the degree to which this competitive pressure spills over into provider markets varies considerably across countries, reflecting the differences in the regulatory environments.[2]

The financing of social health insurance systems is usually based on universal mandatory premiums, based for example on earned income, and independent of a person's expected use of healthcare. This creates a national pool of funds. Each insurer then receives a capitation payment from that fund for each insuree based on characteristics such as the person's age, sex, disability status, and previous medical experience. Such systems therefore require an accurate estimate of the expected annual costs of health care for the individual. This estimate is used to reimburse insurers fairly for the risk profile of their insured populations. In principle, this should ensure that all insurers are able to offer the statutory basic benefits package, thereby assuring equity between insurees and creating what is often referred to as a level playing field for the insurance market. In practice, competitive social insurance schemes have found it challenging to develop accurate risk adjustment mechanisms for use in payment. This has led to the use of a variety of financial protection arrangements that reduce insurers' exposure to the full consequences of inaccurate risk adjustment, but also dampen the market incentives.

In the early stages of development, many schemes adjusted payments for little more than the age and sex of the insuree, a manifestly inadequate approach to assessing expected health care expenditure. More recent efforts have sought to introduce more subtle risk adjustment, for example including characteristics associated with disability status, previous health care utilisation, and employment status. Clearly the introduction of such variables can yield a more accurate estimate of expected expenditure. However, insurers are almost always able to make a more accurate assessment of a potential insuree's expenditure needs than any risk adjustment formula. For example, knowledge of smoking status can rarely be incorporated into a formal risk adjustment formula, because it is not universally recorded (Newhouse, 1994). As well as compromising the efficient and fair operation of the market, this lack of precision gives insurers an incentive to cream skim, that is to seek insurees whom they judge to have lower expected expenditure than implied by the capitation formula, and to discourage enrolment by patients expected to result in high spending. Evidence from Europe suggests that such risk selection activity is increasing in all systems of competitive social health insurance, in spite of formal requirements to accept all applicants for insurance and steady refinements to the risk adjustment processes (van de Ven *et al.*, 2007).

A further problem in any competitive insurance market is the issue of adverse selection – the tendency for higher risk insurees to seek out more generous insurance coverage (Cutler and Zeckhauser, 2000). This arises even under mandatory insurance competition, because insurers offering especially good services for certain services (for example, diabetes care) might attract disproportionate numbers of high-risk patients (in this case, diabetic patients). Unless the capitation scheme properly adjusts for this tendency, insurers have a perverse incentive to offer low quality care (or apparently low quality care) to high-risk patients. Concerns about adverse selection has led to a competitive race to the bottom in US health care, in services for chronic conditions such as mental illness, in order to avoid enrolment of high-risk patients (Wang *et al.*, 2002).

The particular difficulties associated with insurance competition for people with chronic disease have led to an interesting experiment in Germany, where insurance funds are allowed to create disease management programmes for patients who are registered in specific disease groups, the first of which were diabetes, breast cancer, asthma, and coronary heart disease (Busse, 2004). The intention is to define disease-specific minimum standards of care for such groups, which insurers must assure, in return for a raised capitation fee. Numerous issues deserving careful scrutiny and evaluation are raised by this experiment, such as the contents of the programmes, the definition of qualifying patients, and the level of capitation payment.

In order to secure the major benefits of competitive insurance, it is essential that insurers should be able to contract selectively with providers, creating the ability to extract cost efficiencies and quality improvements from the provider market. There is evidence from the US managed-care experience that such selective contracting can yield efficiencies (Glied, 2000). However, only some social insurance systems (such as the Netherlands) allow selective contracting. Where the choice of provider is left to the patient (as in Switzerland), the insurer could become little more than a passive reimburser, limiting the scope for stimulating provider efficiency. The potential gains for insurers are then focused mainly on risk selection activities, which have been especially marked in Germany and Switzerland (van de Ven *et al.*, 2007).

Finally, it is worth noting that a slightly different form of insurance competition relates to the integrated care of a defined population. Examples include the health maintenance organisations such as Kaiser Permanente that have developed in the United States. They exhibit many of the characteristics of a vertically integrated insurance function, in which insurance and service delivery are unified. In practice, they can be viewed as miniature national health systems, albeit embedded within a competitive environment. Thus, the incentives and policy issues they give rise to under competition are similar to those under insurance competition, as discussed above. The main difference is that the provider function is mainly integrated into the same organisation. This may have benefits, in the form of better co-ordinated care and attention to preventive and other public health issues. However, it runs the risk of losing the benefits of a contestable provider market.

Competition for collectively purchased health services

Competition for collective health services arises when a collective purchaser seeks to place block contracts for specified health services, such as hospital-based care, for a defined population group. Although the emphasis in this section is on hospital care, many of the issues apply to other services. The collective purchaser of such services can take a number of forms, including competitive insurers (as in the social health insurance systems discussed above), local governments (as in much of Scandinavia), national or regional health service agencies (as in Italy, Spain, and the United Kingdom), or large employers (as in the United States). Indeed, a major policy development in many tax-funded health systems that were previously vertically integrated has been the deliberate separation of strategic purchasers (such as local health authorities) and providers of care, in order to create markets and competition among providers.

Many strategic purchasers have some choice as to where they place contracts for the collective provision of health services, and so an element of competition between providers arises. As under insurance competition, it is important to note that this type of provider competition arises only if the collective purchaser has some control over where patients receive their treatment. If no such control exists - that is, the choice is determined by the patient or a clinical advisor - competition amongst providers is for individual patients, as discussed in the next section.

In understanding the market for collectively purchased services, one therefore has to understand the objectives and constraints of purchasers. Historically, the purchasing function in health care has been weak (Figueras *et al.*, 2005). Purchasers have either passively reimbursed providers, or based contracts on historical precedent, with little attempt to introduce contestability into the provider market. There is, however, a growing recognition that strategic purchasing must become more active, and that stimulating some sort of competitive market in provision may be an important lever for securing better and more cost-effective services.

Numerous issues arise when considering the functioning of the provider market. Amongst the more important are:

- the nature of the market,
- the contracting process,
- the scope of services to be contracted,
- the duration of the contract,
- any conditions on the nature and costs of services,
- the population to be covered,
- with how many providers to contract,
- the form of reimbursement,
- how prices are to be determined, and
- processes for monitoring contracts.

Although markets are often characterised by the ownership of the competitors (public, private, not-for-profit), their nature should more fundamentally be defined by the incentives operating on the participants. Full-blooded market competition implies free entry and exit, and the ability to retain all financial surpluses. In contrast, the various quasi-markets tested in National Health Service (NHS) types of health system allow public sector providers some freedom to compete for business, but the threats to continued existence are less direct. While these differences may appear minor, they can have a profound influence on the behaviour of market participants. This may be why a comprehensive review of six years' experience of quasi-markets in England concluded "how little overall measurable change there seems to have been related to the core structures and mechanisms of the internal market" (Le Grand, 1998). In short, the quasi-market never offered the competitive pressures implicit in a real market.

The contracting process is another critical element of any market-type process. Contracting may be competitive with separate organisations bidding to provide services. Here several challenges exist. First, it is often infeasible for a purchaser to introduce a realistic competitive threat in the hospital sector, where there are large economies of scale and scope, and therefore few local providers.[3] Second, purchasers rarely explicitly seek out competitive bids. Rather, they more frequently enter into negotiations with existing local providers, seeking to reduce costs or enhance services through a bargaining process. Third, comparable performance measures that can be used to demonstrate the costs or outcomes of services are not well developed. Increasingly, comparative data are being deployed to stimulate what has been termed yardstick competition (Shleifer, 1985). Despite the methodological challenges, in many health systems such comparative data offer the most realistic opportunity to introduce some sort of competition (albeit indirect) into the provider market. Finland has been especially active in promoting benchmarking between hospitals (Noro *et al.*, 2001).

Amongst the most important decisions for a purchaser is the scope of services to be contracted. On the one hand, purchasers could develop multiple markets for different services in order to secure advantageous terms and reap economies of scale by contracting with specialised providers in each sector. However, designing and managing multiple contracting processes introduce high transaction costs. Moreover, it may lead to instability and fragmentation of local health services, and militate against integrated patient care.

Contracting for a broader range of services has a number of benefits, especially in the hospital sector, where there are considerable economies of scope. For example, the provision of emergency services necessarily requires many of the support services also required for outpatient care and elective surgery. Furthermore, contracting with a provider for a broad range of services would allow the purchaser to concentrate its limited contracting capacity on a small number of providers. This one-stop shop approach may also benefit patients, who would not be required to navigate a confusing plurality of providers. Nevertheless, it necessarily results in a narrow range of contracted providers, thereby possibly exacerbating the tendency to local monopoly power of providers, and militating against the emergence of a contestable market. This risk is especially real in more rural areas, where there are often few hospitals.

There is therefore a strong case for adopting a mixed approach to contracting, perhaps using a main provider for the bulk of services, but encouraging contestability for some other hospital services, or for some portion of contracted services. This was achieved (although accidentally) under the general practitioner (GP) arrangement in the United Kingdom, when a main purchaser (the local health authority) was often highly constrained where it could place its main contract, but GP fundholders were free to move some of the health authority's business to other providers if they or their patients preferred (Audit Commission, 1996). This demand-side approach resulted in significantly improved waiting times for patients of GP fundholders (Dusheiko *et al.*, 2004, 2006).

A different approach, based on supply-side policies, has been adopted in England more recently. This has involved the encouragement of a small independent sector to provide competition for the National Health Service at the margin for certain routine surgical procedures, in the form of independent sector treatment centres (ISTCs). A parliamentary scrutiny concluded that "the threat of competition from the ISTCs may have had a significant effect on the NHS, but the evidence is largely anecdotal" (House of Commons Health Committee, 2006). Moreover, the investigation suggested that ISTCs created a number of difficulties, including lack of integration with other health care. A subsequent investigation by the English quality inspectorate found no evidence that ISTCs offered poor quality care (Healthcare Commission, 2007). However, there are persistent concerns that the centres seek healthier patients, and leave the mainstream NHS to pick up the pieces when complications arise (Wallace, 2006).

Collective purchasers will usually be concerned with issues of both effectiveness and cost-effectiveness, which they can promote through the contract monitoring process. Prospectively, they can require adherence to practice guidelines as part of the contract. When the guidelines are widely accepted and known to be associated with good outcomes, this is likely to be an effective mechanism. However, insistence on adherence to process guidelines may stifle the search for innovative delivery mechanisms. Furthermore, where a provider is under contract to several purchasers, a requirement to adhere to a multiplicity of guidelines may increase managerial costs and generate confusion. Increasingly therefore purchasers are looking towards universally accepted patient outcome measures as the means of holding providers accountable.

Although traditional outcome measures, such as post-operative mortality rates, readmission rates and waiting time, can be important signals of clinical quality and responsiveness, they are meaningful for only a small proportion of health services. There is therefore a strong case for purchasers to seek out outcome measures that are useful for a broader range of services. Examples include the patient-reported outcome measures (PROMs) such as EQ5D currently being piloted as performance measures in the English NHS (Office of Health Economics, 2008).

Efficiency measures have a longer tradition of use by purchasers, and form the backbone of many contracting processes. It is worth recalling that the systems of diagnosis-related groups (DRGs), now used as payment mechanisms in many health systems, were originally a mechanism for adjusting for hospital case mix to allow meaningful cost comparison between hospitals (Fetter *et al.*, 1980; Fetter, 1991). Numerous other efficiency indicators exist, such as unit costs (often based on DRGs), length of stay, and day-surgery rates. These are especially important where the scope for real provider competition is limited, and the purchaser must rely on indirect yardstick competition to inform the bargaining process with local providers.

There is quite strong evidence that competition for business from collective health services purchasers has led to cost reductions. In the 1990s, when US providers were preoccupied with competing for contracts from managed-care organisations, unit costs declined significantly (Kessler and McClellan, 2000; Gowrisankaran and Town, 2003). Analogous results have arisen from the period when the English NHS was experimenting with quasi-markets in hospital care (Propper *et al.*, 2008).

Competition could also in principle lead to improvements in other measured aspects of performance that purchasers care about, possibly at the expense of unmeasured aspects of clinical quality. Here the evidence is more ambiguous. In line with predictions, Propper *et al.* (2008) find that competition in England has been associated with lower waiting times (a measured performance indicator of great importance to English purchasers) and worse rates of mortality from acute myocardial infarction (AMI) (a performance indicator that was largely unavailable to purchasers). Martin and Siciliani (2007) confirm the association between competition and improved waiting times, whilst Propper *et al.* (2004) also find a negative association between measures of competition and AMI survival. In contrast, Kessler and McClellan found competition to be associated with improved AMI mortality amongst Medicare patients. This may be because, in contrast to their English counterparts at the time of the studies, US providers also had to attract individual patients, sometimes by offering high-quality infrastructure (see below).

Finally, it is important to note the crucial importance of certain structural incentives, such as the payment mechanism for contracting providers. There are two main forms of payment in widespread use by purchasers: global (fixed) budgets and case payment mechanisms (such as DRG methods). These introduce important incentives for providers. In practice, many providers are funded by a mix of fixed budget (for example, for providing an emergency service) and case payment (for example, for routine surgery). Even where a hospital is apparently funded entirely by a fixed budget, its future budget may nevertheless be influenced by current activity, so there is some link, albeit indirect, between current activity and future reimbursement.

Broadly speaking, the immediate incentives under global budgets are to reduce activity and shift patients to other providers or into the home setting. However, global budgets also encourage cost reduction and secure aggregate expenditure control for the purchaser. In contrast, case payments stimulate increased activity (at least for non-complex patients within any DRG category) and unit cost reduction. Note that neither mechanism in itself stimulates improved quality. (Indeed under global budgets there may be a perverse incentive to reduce quality in order to deter utilisation.) This is leading some purchasers to experiment with so-called pay for performance (P4P) schemes, under which some reimbursement is conditional on reported measures of clinical performance. Although potentially a very interesting development, to date most experiments with P4P have been small scale, and the results inconclusive (Christianson, 2007).

Another important incentive consideration is the existence of market exit arrangements, in the form of a credible threat to the continued existence of market participants. For example, can a payer realistically threaten the continued existence of a district's only hospital? In many health systems, closure of local hospitals is an intensely sensitive political issue, which may be finessed through mechanisms such as mergers with other local hospitals, rather than directly confronted. The design of competitive instruments may need to accommodate this limited scope for market exit, for example by putting the jobs of executives at risk rather than threatening the institution as a whole.

This section has examined the case of competition for health services purchased by collective health purchasers. Devers *et al.* (2003) refer to such markets as a competition for wholesale services, in contrast to the retail market of services sought by individual patients or their clinical advisors. An intermediate situation between competition for collective and individual services arises when purchasers nominate preferred providers that patients are encouraged to use, possibly through the use of additional patient charges for using non-preferred providers. The competition for preferred providers offers elements of wholesale competition, although the incentives are somewhat attenuated by the more conditional nature of the competition to secure preferred provider status. There have been experiments in Switzerland with preferred providers, with about 10% of the population enrolling in insurance schemes under which choice of providers is limited, in exchange for reduced premiums (OECD and WHO, 2006).

Competition for individual health services

The existence of collective health purchasers is to some extent predicated on the desire to constrain, or at least influence, the choice of individual patients in the services they seek and the providers from which they secure treatment. Such constraints are intended to minimise unnecessary use of health care, to assure health care quality, and to promote the use of cost-effective therapies and providers. However, in many health systems patients have traditionally had unfettered access to a basket of approved services offered by any accredited provider. The role of purchaser than becomes mainly one of determining the nature of the health basket, and setting the payment mechanism. The choice of provider (and therefore the attention of the provider market) depends on individual patients and their clinical advisors.

Freedom of patient choice has been a traditional feature of the Bismarckian systems of social health insurance, and the traditional US Medicare system. In such systems there has typically been a plurality of professional providers and provider organisations, and elements of provider competition have been an intrinsic element of the health system. The competition has been mainly on the basis of perceived quality (rather than price), as there is usually a national fixed price tariff for medical treatments, based on DRGs. Through the mandatory insurance arrangements in such systems, patients are protected from most of the immediate expenditure associated with treatment. They therefore have the incentive to seek out health care in excess of efficient levels. This tendency is exacerbated by the incentive for physicians to recommend excessive treatment whenever their income depends on the volume of activity, giving rise to supplier-induced demand (Zweifel and Manning, 2000). As a result, relative to the more collective approach of national health insurance, such systems have in general resulted in good health outcomes, but with relatively high expenditure levels (Normand and Busse, 2002).

An important hypothesis arising within systems of patient choice, developed in the United States in the 1980s, is that competition for patients may give rise to what Robinson and Luft (1987, 1988) have termed a "medical arms race." It argues that, in the absence of accepted outcome measures or other more direct signals of provider quality, providers will compete by offering signals of high-quality care, in the form of advanced technology and superior patient amenities. In its more recent manifestation, the medical arms race hypothesis suggests that providers might adopt strategies such as developing niche specialist services, in order to attract specialists in lucrative services (Devers *et al.*, 2003). Whilst there is some debate about the nature and strength of the medical arms race, there is a strong belief that retail competition for patients may give rise to systematic oversupply of quality and capacity. This belief has even led to some relaxation of US antitrust practice, based on the argument that excessive competition may exacerbate the tendency to oversupply (Federal Trade Commission and US Department of Justice, 2004).

Some of the problems associated with competition for individual patients can be addressed by improved measurement and public reporting of patient outcomes. Whilst there is little evidence to suggest that patients have hitherto paid a great deal of attention to such information, provider organisations (specifically hospitals) are influenced by outcome reporting because of its impact on organisational reputation (Marshall *et al.*, 2003). There is, therefore, some hope that the increased use of performance reporting will incentivise providers to concentrate on aspects of quality that give rise to genuine improvements in patient outcome.

In an attempt to moderate the risk of moral hazard, some social insurance systems have been experimenting with how to make patients more sensitive to the costs associated with their choices. Examples include user charges for access to specialist care in France (Bellanger and Mossé, 2005), discounts on insurance premiums for those not using inpatient care in the Netherlands, and new charges for the first physician encounter in any quarter in Germany (Gericke *et al.*, 2003). These experiments are modest in scope but indicate a desire to give patients some signal of the cost consequences of the care they seek.

In contrast, Beveridge systems, with traditionally more constrained approaches to patient choice, have recently deliberately sought to use markets more actively to promote patient choice and stimulate competition. Such systems have historically offered good cost control while being less responsive to patients' preferences. One purpose for these recent choice initiatives has been to stimulate the entry of new providers into the market, specifically in order to reduce the inpatient waiting times often associated with NHS-type systems (Le Grand, 2007). Typically, these experiments offer patients a guaranteed waiting time, as in Denmark, Sweden or the London Patient Choice Project. If the guarantee is exceeded by the usual provider, patients can seek care from any other accredited provider (Dawson *et al.*, 2007).

More recently, England has offered a different type of choice, under which patients can select from a range of potential providers (nominated by the local health authority) when first referred for specialist investigations. Rather than stimulating the market, the main motivation for this latest initiative appears to be to empower patients, and increase their satisfaction with health services.

Improving policies

Competition exists in different forms in every health system. It may arise directly through the creation of formal markets, but also in less formal or direct ways. One example is the sort of yardstick competition that is created by public performance reporting, which affects provider reputation. This may act to stimulate improvement, both from a business perspective, but also through the natural desire of professionals to be seen to be doing a good job. Furthermore, instruments of competition are already in place in many health systems, such as the traditional freedom of patient choice in social health insurance systems.

Studying the impact of any competition instrument is difficult. Researchers usually rely either on some sort of natural experiment, or on rather crude measures of the magnitude of competitive forces as an explanatory variable. Both these approaches are problematic. There can always be explanations other than competition for the results found in natural experiments. For example, an evaluation of the London Patient Choice Project, designed to reduce waiting times, found faster improvements in waiting time in London than elsewhere, where the experiment was not implemented. However, there may have been many reasons other than the experiment for the differences detected by the researchers. Moreover, measures of competitive forces are often highly correlated with other social or economic conditions. For example, competition is in general weaker in rural areas, so it is difficult to disentangle the specific impact of competition on system behaviour.

There are, nevertheless, some clear messages emerging from the fragmentary evidence described above. First, the policy issues associated with competition in the mandatory insurance market are relatively well understood, and there is an excellent research base emerging from the countries experimenting with this aspect of competition. Promoting competition in the mandatory insurance market is necessarily challenging, given the difficulty of identifying a fair capitation sum for any insuree that accurately reflects his or her expected health care expenditure. Pursuing such insurance competition is likely to require some risk sharing between the insurer and the national payment pool in order to discourage cream skimming. Furthermore, any insurance competition requires an adequate quality assurance process, perhaps in the form of risk-adjusted performance reports for insurers. Given the periodic re-enrolment of insurees, an unresolved issue is how to incentivise insurers to take a longer term perspective, through health promotion and other public health activities. One could create explicit incentives to undertake activities known to be associated with good population health outcomes, or transfer that responsibility to other agencies, such as local governments.

Competition for collectively purchased services is a less clearly defined policy issue. There is diverse experience from the US (contracting between managed care organisations and providers), public sector health services (either quasi-markets in which public sector purchasers contract with public sector providers, or, to an increasing extent, real markets in which there exists a plurality of providers), and social health insurance (with the emergence of preferred provider organisations). The evidence in this domain is rather sparse, much of it from the United States, and it is difficult to draw general conclusions.

Collectively purchased services nevertheless represent the domain that offers most promise for efficiency gains. Collective purchasers in principle have the incentive and capacity to secure improvements in effectiveness and efficiency from a provider market, so long as they are able to contract selectively. The discussion above emphasises the numerous policy decisions that are needed to make competition for collective provider services a reality. These include clarity about the nature of the services for which there is to be competition, the nature of the competitive process, and the reimbursement mechanism. The great variety in these variables makes the comparison and transferability of research results problematic.

There are nevertheless some consistent themes emerging from experience to date. First, the provider market responds to the stated preoccupation of purchasers, whether this is cost containment or some other aspect of performance, such as waiting times. This response may be at the expense of other aspects of health system performance, most notably unmeasured aspects of clinical quality. To mitigate this risk, it is therefore imperative that high quality clinical outcome measurement is implemented alongside any competitive regime. The emerging experience with PROMs is likely to be central to future policy in this domain. Whilst much of the evidence suggests public reporting will stimulate provider improvements, there is also some evidence that it may lead to providers seeking to avoid high-risk patients (Dranove *et al.*, 2003; Hibbard *et al.*, 2005).

Second, the choice of services to be competed for can have profound implications for health system performance. A narrow definition may fragment health care, inhibit the pursuit of integrated care, and reduce the ability of the system to secure economies of scope. However, a broad definition may make it difficult to create a meaningful market, given the high costs of entry. There is scope for experimentation in this domain, and it may be appropriate to employ a mixed strategy, with competition for some clearly defined specialist services alongside a less competitive core health service. Also, the potential for competition for core services through franchise arrangements should be explored.

Third, providers respond to payment mechanisms. Purchasers should therefore examine with some care the way they choose to reimburse providers within a collective market. A mix of fixed and variable budget is likely to be appropriate in most circumstances. However, the exact balance, and the parts of activity that should contribute to the variable element, is an unresolved issue. In the same vein, risk-sharing arrangements are likely to be an important element in securing optimal provider responses, for example in mitigating the incentive for cream-skimming.

From a cost containment perspective, provider competition for individual patients is problematic. The use of case payment (DRG) regimes encourages reductions in unit costs. However, patients and providers have little incentive to economise on the volume of treatments. Some cost sharing between patient and payer may mitigate this effect, but it compromises principles of financial protection. Moreover the RAND experiment suggested that the major losers from this policy are likely to be vulnerable (poor and sick) patients (Newhouse, 1993).

Policy makers seeking to promote increased patient choice need to be clear about whether they are doing so for the intrinsic benefit of patients, or to achieve improved provider performance. If the latter, experience suggests that, unless the desired aspects of performance are properly measured and reported, providers may seek to attract patients by improving the patient experience without necessarily promoting better clinical outcomes. In most cases, some collective approach to purchasing services may be more effective.

Finally, it is important to underline the interconnectedness of competition policy in health care. I have already noted the links between insurance competition and provider competition. Another link, largely outside the scope of this chapter, is the extent of competition in the input markets, most especially pharmaceuticals, capital, and labour. If these input markets are heavily constrained, for example by specified treatment guidelines, existing capital configurations, and national pay structures, then the scope for innovation is much more circumscribed than in less heavily regulated systems. It is probably for this reason that so many health system competition reforms appear to have quite limited impact. Of course there may be good reasons for many of the regulatory instruments put in place, but policy makers cannot expect the same level of impact as would be observed with less heavily regulated input markets.

Conclusions

Competition has obvious attractions for health care policy makers. Markets stimulate providers to maximise long-run profits, and conventional economic theory suggests that, given a satisfactory regulatory framework, they will encourage managerial efficiency, stimulate the entry of new providers when supply is inadequate, lead to efficient contraction in capacity when supply is in surplus, promote quality improvements and innovation, and reduce production costs. Furthermore, decisions about the closure and reconfiguration of providers will be delegated to the market, absolving policy makers of direct responsibility for what are often highly contentious changes.

When considering the role of competition in health care, the question is not whether markets work perfectly, but whether some sort of market-type organisation leads to better outcomes than other forms of organisation, and what the best form of such organisation might be. Conventional neoclassical economic thinking predicts this will occur by markets driving down costs and improving outcomes to efficient levels. But there are other more radical views of markets. For example, the Austrian school considers the prime benefit of market organisation is the incentives it offers for rent seeking and opportunistic behaviour. From this perspective, the prime virtue of market-type organisation is fostering innovation.

In contrast, the sociological viewpoint is that all economic action is socially situated, and is embedded in networks of social relations. Individual actors are rarely, if ever, autonomous and, any health system is shaped by institutions, power relations, networks and common practices. This implies that the success or otherwise of any market-based initiative is likely to be highly contingent on the institutional and cultural setting within which it is implemented (Smith *et al.*, 2005). From this perspective, market-type arrangements are therefore constructed realities in which society (or those engaged in transactions) decide *1)* what can be completed over or not, *2)* who can buy and sell, and *3)* how transactions will take place. Thus, the rules and boundaries of market exchange should be scrutinised in order to understand the roles and functions of purchasers that society wants to develop. In particular, one would attend to relations between powerful buyers and sellers (or their agents) in order to assess how their relations affect their economic behaviour.

Whatever perspective is adopted, it is clear that competition is becoming a central instrument of health policy. However, for most aspects of the health system, there is currently little unequivocal evidence on which to base such policy. There are, nevertheless, certain general lessons that can be drawn from the emerging evidence on the role of markets and competition in health care.

The first is that competition in health care, of whatever nature, requires careful policy design. Even if immediate objectives are secured, it is likely that unintended side-effects will compromise other heath system objectives. In short, any market experiment should be designed with monitoring and evaluation clearly in mind, so that the research base can be enhanced and future policy refined and amended accordingly.

Second, for any policy maker, the point of departure is usually the existing set of institutional arrangements, which will usually already contain some elements of competition. For example, most systems already allow some choice about where patients receive treatment, and many providers therefore have at least some incentive to attend to competitive pressures. A failure to capture sufficient business would at the very least expose a provider's management to awkward questions about its performance. However, the precise incentives in place can vary considerably, and even subtle variations in institutional settings can give rise to different outcomes. Therefore, policy makers should ask not "what works", but "what works in what setting?"

Third, on its own, competition cannot succeed in delivering policy objectives. Other policy instruments need to be correctly aligned to make competition stand a chance of success. These may include the financing mechanism, the performance measurement regime, and entry and exit mechanisms. All health care markets are quite properly heavily regulated; the regulatory rules should to be carefully aligned with objectives in order to ensure competition results in the desired outcomes.

Fourth, competition should be implemented with care. Markets can produce great instability, variations in performance, and inequalities. Many health systems, especially those espousing principles of solidarity, set great store by promoting equity and comprehensive health care. Continual vigilance and oversight is necessary to ensure that such health system objectives are not being compromised. Effective implementation of market-type mechanisms is therefore likely to require considerable managerial skills and impose substantial transaction costs, particularly in purchasing and regulatory institutions.

Fifth, the perils associated with competition are likely to be relatively immaterial for some acute aspects of care with homogenous patient groups, for which there are good measures of outcome and well-understood technologies. Well-managed competition undoubtedly confers many benefits alongside the challenges sketched out above, and so there is a case for experimenting with the careful introduction of sharper competitive pressures for such interventions, particularly if purchased collectively. Yet even such modest experimentation runs the risk of focusing managers' attention on the competitive sector, at the expense of other services, most notably the non-acute sector. It is difficult to envisage circumstances in which a truly competitive market can be created for many common (and costly) chronic conditions with heterogeneous patient groups, for which there are few if any measures of outcome, complex patient pathways, and high reliance on interactions with other agencies, such as social care agencies.

Finally, the evidence base for setting policy in this domain remains feeble, and there is a pressing need for more and better research to understand better the nature of competition, the circumstances in which it works, the methods of maximising its effectiveness, and the lessons for policy.

In short, true market competition introduces a set of raw incentives that carry serious potential for adverse outcomes for many aspects of health care. However, competition can take many different forms, and sharpening competitive forces is likely in general to be an important tool for most health systems. Policy makers nevertheless need to shape market-type mechanisms with care, to align other policy levers, and to monitor vigilantly, in order to maximise the benefits they secure.

Notes

1. Thanks to Howard Oxley, Ian Brownwood, Francesca Colombo, Elizabeth Docteur and Peter Scherer for their help in preparing this chapter.
2. For example, competitive insurance markets in the Netherlands allow insurers to selectively negotiate with providers for ambulatory care and for approximately 10% of institutional care. In Switzerland, providers and insurers negotiate as groups in a bilateral monopoly environment and selective contracting and price setting are not allowed.
3. Another perhaps more feasible approach would, therefore, be to contract competitively for the franchise to run local hospital services.

Bibliography

Audit Commission (1996), *What the Doctor Ordered: A Study of GP Fundholders in England and Wales*, HMSO, London.

Bellanger, M. and P. Mossé (2005), "The Search for the Holy Grail: Combining Decentralised Planning and Contracting Mechanisms in the French Health Care System", *Health Economics*, Vol. 14, No. S1, pp. S119-S132.

Busse, R. (2004), "Disease Management Programs in Germany's Statutory Health Insurance System", *Health Affairs*, Vol. 23, No. 3, pp. 56-67.

Christianson, J. (2007), *Financial Incentives, Healthcare Providers and Quality Improvements. A Review of the Evidence*, Health Foundation, London.

Colombo, F. and N. Tapay (2004), "Private Health Insurance in OECD Countries: The Benefits and Costs for Individuals and Health Systems", OECD Health Working Papers, No. 15, OECD Publishing, Paris.

Cutler, D. and R. Zeckhauser (2000), "The Anatomy of Health Insurance", in J.P. Newhouse and A.J. Culyer (eds.), *Handbook of Health Economics*, Elsevier, Amsterdam.

Dawson, D. *et al.* (2007), "The Effects on Waiting Times of Expanding Provider Choice: Evidence from a Policy Experiment", *Health Economics*, Vol. 16, No. 2, pp. 113-128.

Devers, K., L. Brewster and L. Casalino (2003), "Changes in Hospital Competitive Strategy: A New Medical Arms Race?", *Health Services Research*, Vol. 38, No. 1, pp. 447-469.

Dranove, D. *et al.* (2003), "Is More Information Better? The Effects of 'Report Cards' on Health Care Providers", *Journal of Political Economy*, Vol. 111, No. 3, pp. 555-588.

Dusheiko, M., H. Gravelle and R. Jacobs (2004), "The Effect of Practice Budgets on Patient Waiting Times: Allowing for Selection Bias", *Health Economics*, Vol. 13, No. 10, pp. 941-958.

Dusheiko, M. *et al.* (2006), "The Effect of Budgets on Doctor Behaviour: Evidence from a Natural Experiment", *Journal of Health Economics*, Vol. 25, pp. 449-478.

Federal Trade Commission and U.S. Department of Justice (2004), *Improving Healthcare: A Dose of Competition*, Washington DC.

Fetter, R. (1991), "Diagnosis Related Groups: Understanding Hospital Performance", *Interfaces*, Vol. 21, No. 1, pp. 6-26.

Fetter, R. *et al.* (1980), "Case Mix Definition by Diagnosis-Related Groups", *Medical Care*, Vol. 18, No. 2, pp. 1-53.

Figueras, J., R. Robinson and E. Jakubowski (2005), *Purchasing to Improve Health Systems Performance*, Open University Press, Maidenhead.

Gericke, C., M. Wismar and R. Busse (2003), "Cost-Sharing in the German Health Care System", Discussion Paper, Department of Health Care Management, Technische Universität Berlin, Berlin.

Glied, S. (2000), "Managed Care", in J.P. Newhouse and A.J. Culyer (eds.), *Handbook of Health Economics*, Elsevier, Amsterdam.

Gowrisankaran, G. and R.J. Town (2003), "Competition, Payers, and Hospital Quality", *Health Services Research*, Vol. 38, No. 6, pp. 1403-1422.

Healthcare Commission (2007), *Independent Sector Treatment Centres A Review of the Quality of Care*, Healthcare Commission, London.

Hibbard, J.H., J. Stockard and M. Tusler (2005), "Hospital Performance Reports: Impact on Quality, Market Share, And Reputation", *Health Affairs*, Vol. 24, No. 4, pp. 1150-1160.

House of Commons Health Committee (2006), *Independent SectorTreatment Centres. Fourth Report of Session 2005–06*, House of Commons, London.

Kessler, D. and M. McClellan (2000), "Is Hospital Competition Socially Wasteful?", *Quarterly Journal of Economics*, Vol. 115, No. 2, pp. 577-615.

Le Grand, J. (2007), *The Other Invisible Hand: Delivering Public Services through Choice and Competition*, Princeton University Press, Princeton, NJ.

Le Grand, J., N. Mays and J. Mulligan (1998), *Learning from the NHS Internal Market*, King's Fund Institute, London.

Marshall, M. *et al.* (2003), "Public Reporting on Quality: Lessons from the United States and the United Kingdom", *Health Affairs*, Vol. 22, No. 3, pp. 134-148.

Martin, S. and L. Siciliani (2007), "An Empirical Analysis of the Impact of Choice on Waiting Times", *Health Economics*, Vol. 16, No. 8, pp. 763-779.

Newhouse, J. (1993), *Free for All? Lessons from the RAND Health Insurance Experiment*, Harvard University Press, Cambridge, MA.

Newhouse, J. (1994), "Patients at Risk: Health Reform and Risk Adjustment", *Health Affairs*, Vol. 13, No. 1, pp. 135-146.

Normand, C. and R. Busse (2002), "Social Health Insurance Financing", in E. Mossialos, A. Dixon, J. Figueras and J. Kutzin (eds.), *Funding Health Care: Options for Europe*, Open University Press, Buckingham.

Noro, A. *et al.* (2001), *Implementation of RAI-instruments and Benchmarking the Care of the Elderly,* Stakes Aiheita 17/2001, STAKES, Helsinki.

OECD Health Project (2004), *Private Health Insurance in OECD Countries*, OECD Publishing, Paris.

OECD and World Health Organisation (2006), *OECD Reviews of Health Systems: Switzerland*, OECD Publishing, Paris.

Office of Health Economics (2008), *Report of the Office of Health Economics Commission on NHS Outcomes, Performance and Productivity*, OHE, London.

Propper, C., S. Burgess and D. Gossage (2008), "Competition and Quality: Evidence from the NHS Internal Market 1991-9", *Economic Journal*, Vol. 118, pp. 138-170.

Propper, C., S. Burgess and C. Green (2004), "Does Competition Between Hospitals Improve the Quality of Care? Hospital Death Rates and the NHS Internal Market", *Journal of Public Economics*, Vol. 88, No. 7-8, pp. 1247-1272.

Robinson, J.C. and H.S. Luft (1987), "Competition and the Cost of Hospital Care, 1972–1982", *Journal of the American Medical Association*, Vol. 257, No. 23, pp. 3241-3245.

Robinson, J.C. and H.S. Luft (1988), "Competition and the Cost of Hospital Care, 1982-1986", *Journal of the American Medical Association*, Vol. 260, No. 18, pp. 2676-2681.

Shleifer, A. (1985), "A Theory of Yardstick Competition", *Rand Journal of Economics*, Vol. 16, No. 3, pp. 319-327.

Smith, P. (2000), *Reforming Markets in Health Care: An Economic Perspective*, Open University Press, Buckingham.

Smith, P. *et al.* (2005), "Role of Markets and Competition", in J. Figueras, R. Robinson and E. Jakubowski (eds.), *Purchasing to Improve Health Systems Performance*, Open University Press, Maidenhead.

van de Ven, W. *et al.* (2003), "Risk Adjustment and Risk Selection in the Sickness Fund Insurance Market in Five European Countries", *Health Policy*, Vol. 65, No. 1, pp. 75-98.

van de Ven, W. *et al.* (2007), "Risk Adjustment and Risk Selection in Europe: Six Years Later", *Health Policy*, Vol. 83, No. 2-3, pp. 162-179.

Wallace, W. (2006), "Independent Sector Treatment Centres: How the NHS is Left to Pick Up the Pieces", *British Medical Journal*, Vol. 332, p. 614.

Wang, P., O. Demler and R. Kessler (2002), "Adequacy of Treatment for Serious Mental Illness in the United States", *American Journal of Public Health*, Vol. 92, No. 1, pp. 92-98.

Zweifel, P. and W. Manning (2000), "Moral Hazard and Consumer Incentives in Health Care", in J.P. Newhouse and A.J. Culyer (eds,), *Handbook of Health Economics*, Elsevier, Amsterdam.

Chapter 3.

Improving Health Care System Performance through Better Co-ordination of Care

By Howard Oxley,
Formerly of the Health Division, OECD

This chapter provides a broad overview of care coordination issues and approaches in OECD and European Union (EU) countries. It also looks at how health care systems are responding to the increasing prevalence of chronic disease and the scope for improved health system performance through enhanced policies in this area.

Introduction

Can better care co-ordination within health and long-term care systems improve health system performance in terms of quality and cost-efficiency? This chapter provides a broad overview of care co-ordination issues and approaches in OECD countries and European Union countries that are not OECD members. It examines how health care systems are responding to the increasing prevalence of chronic disease and assesses whether and how OECD and EU countries might improve the performance of their health systems in this area.

Broadly speaking, co-ordination of care is a technique for ensuring that individual patients get both appropriate care for acute episodes and care to stabilise their health over longer periods in less costly environments. Such co-ordination is particularly important for patients with chronic conditions and the elderly who may have difficulty navigating fragmented health care systems or who may need of long-term institutional care. While care co-ordination policies come in different forms, they mainly aim at improving continuity of care for individual patients and reducing the need for high-cost hospital stays. Thus, they should both increase quality and reduce cost of care. While some form of co-ordination exists in most countries, there is room for improvement and the chapter identifies some of the key impediments to better policies in this area, largely drawing on questionnaire replies from 26 countries (see Box 3.1). However, the assessment of the cost effectiveness of such policies is hampered by the limited amount of evidence regarding their impact. In this context, particular attention is given to so-called "targeted" programmes, primarily of a disease or case management nature, as these policies are being introduced in a growing number of countries as one type of care co-ordination programme.

Interest in co-ordination of care issues is increasing

Increased interest in co-ordination of care issues reflects the epidemiological shift from communicable disease towards chronic conditions. Scattered data from a number of countries indicate that individuals with chronic conditions tend to be high users of health care services and have numerous contacts with the health care system. Thus, efforts to control costs should ensure that these high-cost groups are obtaining the most cost-efficient care. Survey responses from national health authorities surveyed by OECD indicate that policy makers in virtually all responding countries were concerned about inadequate care co-ordination. Almost 80% of respondents see patients with chronic conditions and the elderly as being the population groups likely to be most affected by inadequate co-ordination of care.

Since most of the chronically ill are elderly, the importance of chronic conditions will likely increase over the next 30 years as populations age.[1] This outcome will depend, among other things, on *1)* future behaviour affecting health risks; *2)* advances in medicine and their costs; and *3)* the effects of lengthening lifetimes.[2] Even though healthy lifetimes are expected to lengthen over the coming years, thereby putting off high death-related health care costs into the future, increased health spending may be necessary to delay the onset of disease, to palliate its eventual chronic effects, and to allow the population to benefit from better technology.

Box 3.1. OECD questionnaire on co-ordination of care

With consistent cross-country information on care co-ordination largely absent, the OECD's Secretariat used a questionnaire to canvass views and gather information on current care-co-ordination concerns, problems, and practices in OECD countries and others belonging to the European Union. This questionnaire, for which responses were received from 26 countries, covered four areas: the importance of co-ordination issues and population groups affected; co-ordination practices; impediments to care co-ordination and the importance of targeted programmes in their country. Responses to specific statements or questions in the questionnaire use a Likert scale in order to capture the intensity of concerns or the frequency of occurrence of certain problems, policies or events.* In this case, a scale of one to three was used with a label attached to each level (*e.g.* seldom, moderately frequent, often).

Given the range of government departments, agencies, and professional bodies involved in monitoring and promoting care co-ordination, countries were encouraged to enlist the help of a range of stakeholders at different governmental and professional levels in answering the questionnaire. For federal countries, the Secretariat recommended that the federal or central authorities prepare the questionnaire, drawing on expertise at the sub-national level where available. (For further information, see Annex 2 of Hofmarcher *et al.*, 2007.)

* A Likert scale is a rating scale designed to measure attitudes or reactions by quantifying subjective information. Participants indicate where along a continuum their attitude or reaction resides. Likert scales are widely used in social research, including health services research. Usually, three to seven responses (*i.e.*, degrees of frequency or intensity of agreement) are used. The precision increases with the number of elements in the scale.

Several features of existing health care systems have contributed to problems of care co-ordination. For most countries, health care delivery occurs in a series of separate care settings, sometimes referred to as silos. These can be institutionally independent and often operate under different budgetary regimes, particularly where they are under the responsibility of different levels of government. At the same time, medical knowledge has become increasingly specialised, partly reflecting technological change.

These factors may make it more difficult for the chronically ill to find their way through the system.

This chapter reviews information from the questionnaire and the literature on care-co-ordination problems and issues. It then describes care co-ordination programmes focusing on disease and case management. The final section reviews how care co-ordination might be improved by broader changes to the health care system.

Care co-ordination: issues, practices and concerns

Analysis of the results from the OECD survey and the literature more generally suggests that concern over care co-ordination issues is widespread among policy makers, health care providers, and the public at large. These concerns appear to be more intense in countries with high levels of health care spending relative to gross domestic product (GDP). Replies to the questionnaire also overwhelmingly indicate that policy discussions about care co-ordination are most closely linked to issues of quality of care (*i.e.*, that is the impact on health outcomes and responsiveness to patient needs), cost efficiency and, to a lesser degree, ensuring access to care. Concern over quality of care reflects the wide body of research pointing to care that does not meet best practice standards. For example, Asch *et al.* (2006) estimate that half of patients in the United States do not receive the care they should, a result that echoes in the report *Crossing the Quality Chasm* (Kohn *et al.*, 2000). A large number of studies also indicate that there are important differences in practice patterns and new data suggest that there are high levels of medical error in other countries as well (Schoen *et al.*, 2005; Docteur and Oxley, 2003).

The survey results suggest that there are a number of common features of care co-ordination practices across the OECD and the European Union:

- Irrespective of whether there are gatekeeping arrangements, nearly all countries have some form of regulatory or behavioral constraint on referrals. In the view of the questionnaire respondents, first contacts with the health care system almost always occur at the primary care level and patients do not often see specialist without a referral (Figure 3.1).

- More than half of countries see primary care providers as "often" giving patients guidance as they move through the health care system (Figure 3.2). They thereby act, to some degree at least, as care co-ordinators. However, the role of the primary care physicians in guiding the patient appears to decline in many countries as patients move towards hospital and institutional care.[3]

- Respondents suggest that referrals from hospitals back to primary care providers are widespread, possibly reflecting the importance attributed to primary care providers in ensuring patient follow-up and care co-ordination (Figure 3.1).[4] Referrals from hospitals back to ambulatory care specialists are less frequent; this pattern of referrals and the resulting provider behavior seem to be a key source of concern for national authorities with respect to co-ordination of care.

- Particular problems in co-ordination appear at the interfaces between levels of care, especially at cross-over points to long-term care (Figure 3.3). Around two thirds of countries reported that they agree with the statement that difficulties exist at transitions from ambulatory care and four fifths at the level of transitions from acute care. In spite of the fact that other health care professionals are managing transitions into long-term care, these services are not adequate or appropriately formulated to meet the challenge of care co-ordination. These problems seem to prevail in spite of widespread efforts in many countries to improve continuity between hospital and community care (Leichsenring *et al.*, 2004).[5]

- In comparison, problems within care settings seem less important (Figure 3.3). For example, care co-ordination within hospitals is carried out most of the time at the specialist level. Nonetheless, 30% of countries indicate problems of care co-ordination within hospitals, suggesting that there is also potential to improve the organisation of care delivery in hospitals.

- Financing of care from multiple sources that are tied to individual silos can make care co-ordination more difficult and encourage cost shifting between provider levels; and,

- Co-ordination of care may be hampered where strong limitations exist on scope of practice rules of different health care professionals and where there is a lack of mutual professional esteem between them.

Figure 3.1. Who refers patients?

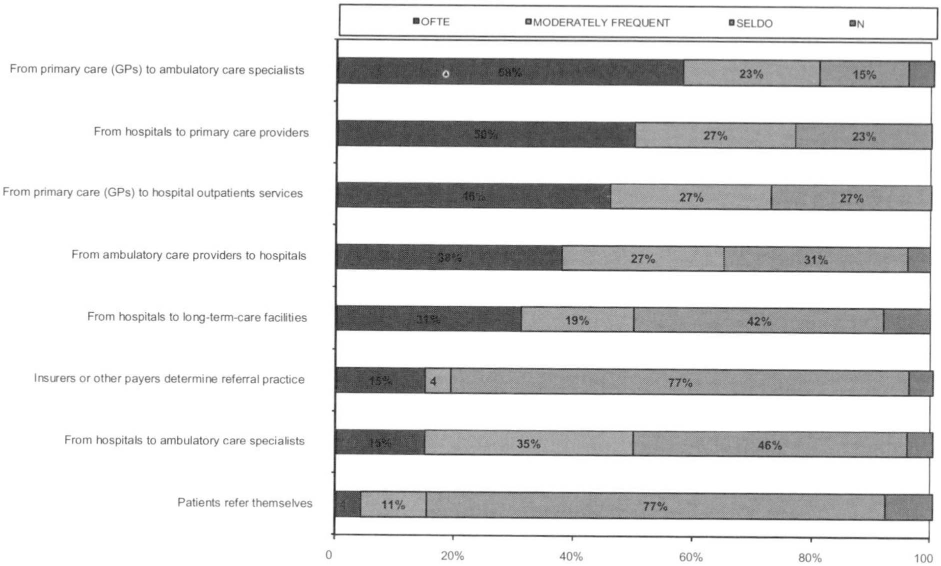

Source: OECD questionnaire on co-ordination of care 2006.

Figure 3.2. Who refers patients?

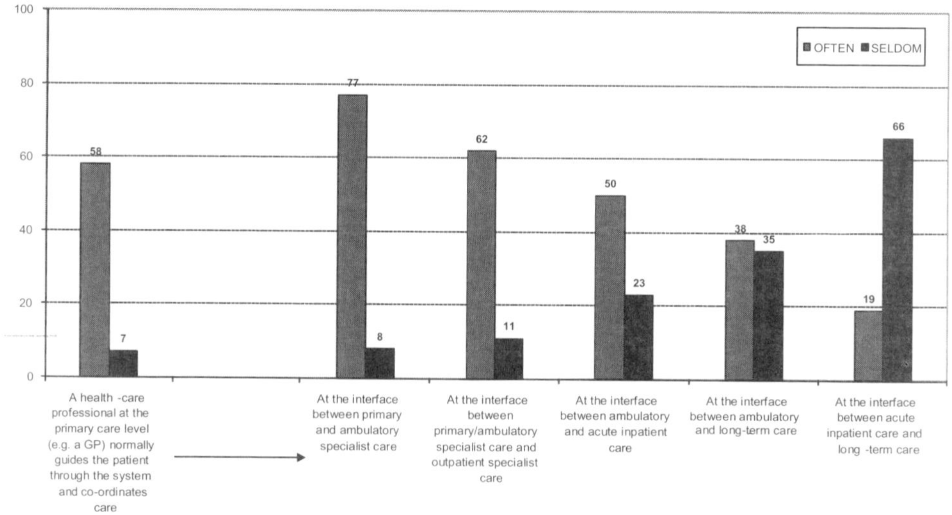

Source: OECD questionnaire on co-ordination of care 2006.

Figure 3.3. Where do problems of care co-ordination occur?

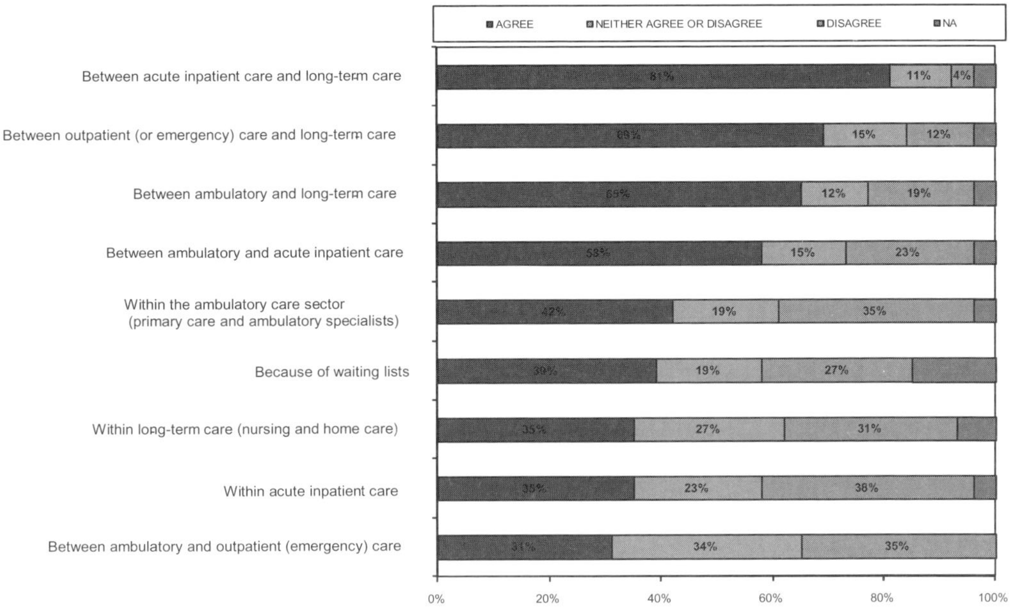

Source: OECD questionnaire on co-ordination of care 2006.

In sum, replies to the questionnaire provide a fairly consistent picture across countries of some form of care co-ordination in which health professionals help guide patients across institutional transitions and within individual sectors. However, country replies to the questionnaire also suggest that the health-care "co-ordinator" can, and often does, differ at each transition, such that there is no assurance that patients are followed by a sole health-care professional through any single episode of care.

Despite the recognised importance of co-ordination of care, few countries encourage it on a contractual basis (Figure 3.4). Only 31% of countries report that they "often" have explicit payment for care co-ordination at the primary care level. Care co-ordination objectives or stipulations regarding care quality are even less frequent. Thus, there is little financial encouragement for improved care co-ordination even though co-ordination takes time and needs to be rewarded if it is not to be crowded out by remunerated activities.

Figure 3.4. Arrangements and incentives for care co-ordination

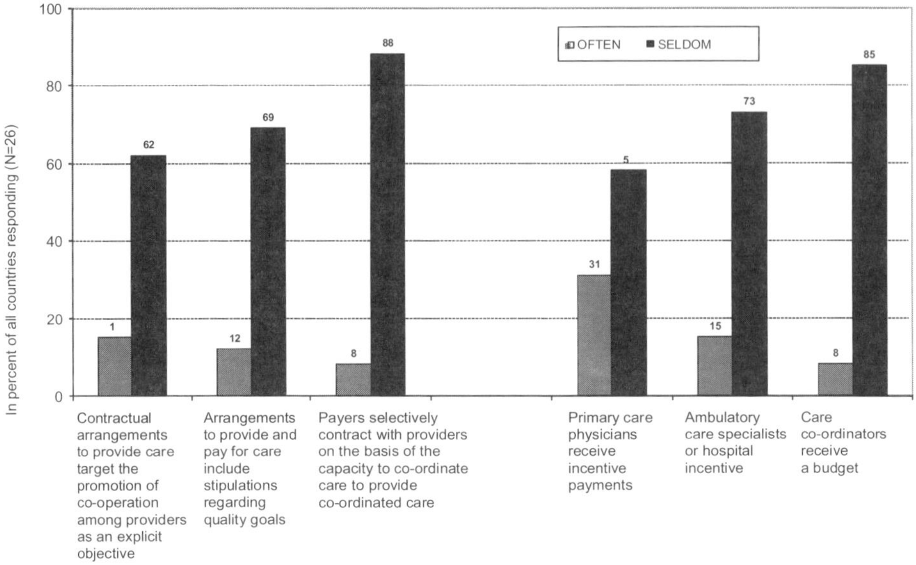

Source: OECD questionnaire on co-ordination of care 2006.

In many cases, current structures do not encourage the development of skills aimed at chronic care management, communication with patients, patient support, and networking with other providers, particularly in the social- or long-term care sectors. Some studies suggest that time allocated to see patients can differ significantly across countries and between the predominant payment schemes in use.[6] Only a small fraction of countries has given their primary care co-ordinators budgets to purchase care for their patients.

Targeted care programmes and their impact

Much policy attention has been focused in recent years on targeted programmes, such as disease and case management that focus on a specific illness or population group. These programmes are intended to increase the quality of care through better follow-up of patients with chronic conditions with the expectation of reducing unplanned hospital stays and the use of emergency services. The questionnaire examined the extent of these programmes; this was supplemented by a literature review of practices and outcomes in the United States (where these programmes were first introduced in a major way) and in Germany and the United Kingdom where reforms in this direction have been more recent.

Box 3.2. How disease management works: an example from the United States

Disease and case management programmes in the United States are now largely provided by specialist firms under contract to insurance companies. These companies first attempt to identify at-risk patients, drawing on clinical and other data in the client's (insurer's) files. Once these patients are enrolled, they are followed by case co-ordinators, case managers or disease managers with the level of follow-up depending on the risk of complications.* Patients are contacted most often via telephone to assess needs and to ensure that best practices in medical care are being followed. These programmes tend to have only limited direct contact with the patient's doctor, even where a problem requiring rapid medical intervention has been identified. Disease or case managers often can only recommend that the patient contact her or his physician or an emergency department. Direct contact, where it exists, can take the form of home visits (rather rare), various forms of electronic medical checks at distance, co-ordination of hospital care in the case of hospital admission, and programmes of transition management aimed at reducing risks when patients move from acute to long-term care settings.

* The largest of these service providers (American Healthways) finds that 3% to 5% of patients with chronic conditions require case management. Normally, there is 1case manager (usually a nurse) for a maximum of 100 patients. Disease management programmes cover 20% to 40% of the patients and are followed by one nurse for every 700 patients. Remaining individuals are mainly provided with education services to enhance their capacity for self-help and self-care (IGAS, 2006).

Source: Howe (2005) as cited by IGAS (2006).

Questionnaire replies and the review of the three country cases revealed a range of policy and market-driven approaches. For example, the United States and, to a lesser extent, Germany has focused on programmes largely operating in parallel with the existing provider arrangements. In contrast, British disease and care management programmes appear to be more tightly bound into the existing general practitioner (GP) arrangements, as has been the case in some larger health maintenance organisations (HMOs) in the United States. Some additional countries have begun to establish such programmes and others are experimenting with such arrangements but they remain at a very early stage, often in the form of pilots. Only one quarter of the reporting countries indicated programmes of this nature and these most frequently concern diabetes.[7]

Assessing whether such programmes have the desired impact on performance is not straightforward. There are large differences between the programmes in terms of structure and intent. Evaluations differ due to the length of time of the trials and in the methodology used for evaluation. The bulk of the information comes from the United States, where the institutional environment for finance and provision of health care differs from most other countries. While it is probably too early to take a definitive view of their effects, it would appear, nonetheless, that these programmes have an impact on quality of care although the impact can depend on the illness in question.

There is less evidence that these programmes always lead to significant and observable cost savings. Although some studies have found positive results and these appear stronger for some pathologies than for others, the results are not consistently positive. A recent review of the literature suggests that gains in short-term cost efficiency are more likely for heart disease, chronic obstructive pulmonary disease, and kidney failure (IGAS, 2006). These results need to be treated with caution as all costs may not have been taken into account in assessing cost efficiency. The effects on cost efficiency remain less clear for diabetes. Benefits in the form of reduced blood-sugar levels are significant, but the impact on cost efficiency may depend on the longer term development and cost of such programmes. Programmes for asthma, depression and back pain do not appear to be cost effective (although there are positive effects on process indicators). However, these results have essentially concerned individuals under 65 in the United States and it is by no means certain that they can be generalised to the elderly taken as a group or to other countries.

There are several possible reasons why programmes do not seem to always result in cost savings: high costs of setting up and operating programmes; the fact that these programmes may reveal unmet needs; and, inadequate matching of care and follow-up with the degree of need. The latter can be technically difficult, particularly where there is only limited clinical or other information (such as the degree of family support) available for this purpose. To achieve consistently better performance of health care systems, such targeted programmes may need to be developed within broader efforts to improve care co-ordination and to make care delivery more patient-centred.

Estimates of returns on investment may, however, need to go beyond a narrow definition of cost savings. Improvements in quality of care are valuable in their own right while the net overall impact on costs can be more important if costs were adjusted, for example, to take into account the number of working days lost due to illness. Indeed, Liljas and Ladensuo (1997) find much higher rates of return, for Sweden, once they take into account the number of days of reduced activity as a result of the disease. In addition, programmes that lead to longer lifetimes should include a valuation of these gains (for example, in the form of quality-adjusted life years). Policy makers may need to take into account the positive social effects from better health and more complete care for those with chronic illness in assessing whether to embark on such programmes. More research is certainly needed on the impact of these programmes using common definitions, analytical methods and time frames.

IGAS (2006) also suggests three broad conditions that appear likely to increase the chances of a positive result: *1)* where providers are more integrated – either in physician group network models, in staff model HMOs such as Kaiser Permanente or in the US Veterans Health Administration;[8] *2)* where other medical personnel such as nurses or social workers and pharmacists are integrated into the care process and follow-up; and, *3)* where programmes encourage patients to change their behaviour through patient education and self-help. Indeed, programmes which combine both patient education and a stronger role of other medical personnel than doctors seem to reinforce each other and have a stronger overall impact.[9]

In sum, disease management programmes have the potential to improve health outcomes and to raise system performance in terms of quality even if the impact on costs remains uncertain. However, these models are only one approach to enhancing care co-ordination. Recent policies in a number of countries are also seeking to provide appropriate and safe care outside of hospitals by strengthening the role of ambulatory care delivery. Thus, more attention may need to be paid to ensuring that information flows, care capacity, incentives, and patterns of provision in the ambulatory sector are adequate to support such changes.

Policies for system-wide improvements in care co-ordination

Questionnaire results suggest that four key policy areas are critical for achieving improvements in care co-ordination and in overall health-care system performance. These are:

- improved information technology and communication infrastructure for information transfer;
- evaluation of the adequacy of the resources devoted to ambulatory and primary care;
- reconfiguring provider systems and incentives to enhance care co-ordination, and
- breaking down barriers between levels and components of care.

The wide variation in the starting positions of individual countries implies that the precise mix of policies will necessarily depend on the institutional framework of the country in question.

Better collection and transmission of information is needed

The need for better information flows is the most widely debated care co-ordination issue across OECD countries. Improved collection and dissemination of information on patients and provider performance is essential to improved system performance. Organisation of referrals and the appropriateness of care are facilitated if patient information is recent, accurate and provided on a timely basis. System governance and improvement of the quality of care also depend on having up-to-date indicators of provider performance.

While information and communications technology (ICT) appears to hold promise as a vehicle for this purpose, the penetration of information technology is weak in many countries despite increased government efforts and significantly improved technology. Questionnaire results show that information on medical records and patient needs is "often" shared among providers in only half of the countries. On the basis of the OECD questionnaire, scarcely 15% of countries consider that providers are "often" equipped with information technology (IT) and only about one third "often" have patient files in electronic format. Countries also consider that the transmission of information on quality of care is infrequent (12% of countries "agree"), very likely reflecting the fact that many countries do not yet collect information on quality at the practitioner level.

Despite this increased interest from policy makers and reduced resistance from patient and consumer groups (who remain, nonetheless, concerned about confidentiality issues), ICT systems can be expensive, requiring heavy up-front investment and non-negligible operating and maintenance costs. Since benefits may often accrue only in the medium- to long-term, judging where the marginal benefits from increased information availability and transfer are highest is likely to be difficult.

Building adequate capacity in care settings outside acute hospital care

Most countries have experienced a shift in delivery from an inpatient to an outpatient environment. As mentioned, these developments seem likely to become more accentuated as populations' age over coming decades. However, doing so without declines in quality and effectiveness requires adequate ICT resources for individual ambulatory care providers and systems that permit the transmission of information among providers. In this context, governments may need to consider whether the relative share of overall resources allocated to the ambulatory sector is in line with the new patterns of demand. In the limited number of countries for which data is available, the share of total health-care spending absorbed by ambulatory care providers has not, on average, substantially increased over the last decade. In such cases, a reassessment of the balance of financial resources going to the various care sectors may be needed.

Such assessments would need, of course, to be taken in conjunction with an analysis of the appropriateness of existing models of ambulatory care provision and the mode of provider payment. Responses to the questionnaire suggest that, in general, co-ordination of care is not limited by the supply of health care professionals, even where the supply of doctors is limited. However, a majority of countries noted that restrictions on the scope of professional activities of providers other than physicians can limit their capacity to undertake care-co-ordination activities.

Cost-effectiveness may be enhanced if a new classification of medical workers were dedicated to undertaking co-ordination. A European study found that the management of patients at transitions to long-term care was facilitated if the care models had included a clear statement that co-ordination/integration is a task on its own, with respective skills and methods, that is, co-ordination as a profession (Leichsenring *et al.*, 2004). In this context, the promotion of a shared culture in teams has been found to mitigate some of the resistance of medical providers towards multidisciplinary work (Coxon *et al.*, 2004). Thus, profiles of health-care professionals and, in particular, of medical professionals involved in co-ordinating care need to be adapted to the multifaceted challenge of curing and caring for chronically ill patients.

Better ambulatory care models for better care co-ordination are needed

Third, and possibly more important, policy makers may need to adapt their ambulatory care models to the new demands placed on them by chronic diseases. While there is often a presumption that primary care providers are best placed to take on this role, multidisciplinary teams involving medical and non-medical professionals may, in fact, be better at providing more coherent care, particularly for patients with multiple pathologies. Systems dominated by providers operating in solo practice and paid for on a fee-for-service basis may be less-well suited to meeting the care needs of the chronically ill.

In practice, referral patterns show that most countries appear to channel, in one way or another, the entry of patients into the health-care system via the primary care provider. Questionnaire replies of most countries indicate that access to specialist care, in either ambulatory or in-patient environments, is normally associated with a primary care referral. Thus, there is some presumption that the primary caregiver is possibly best placed to undertake this co-ordinating task, even though the questionnaire replies also suggest that the role of the primary care provider weakens as patients move (as dictated by their conditions) to progressively more intensive levels of care. This, in turn, may require encouraging multidisciplinary teams to be involved and, in this context, attention needs to be paid to whether GPs have the capacity or willingness to take on this task.

A number of issues arise concerning the nomination of care co-ordinators and the incentives to encourage greater co-ordination. For countries wishing to build on existing care structures, a care co-ordinator with an appropriate professional profile would need to be identified. The questionnaire results suggest that this is often not done. For most countries, the primary care provider is the person usually presumed to provide co-ordination. But there is no necessary reason why co-ordination of care should always be at the primary care level. Indeed, recent French reforms permit specialists to be named as family doctors who may act as care co-ordinators.[10] One potential concern is whether primary care doctors have the necessary skills to operate as care co-ordinator, especially in countries where there has been no tradition for treating general medicine as a specialisation in its own right.

In addition, there are a wide range of primary care models to choose from among respondent countries, some of which may provide more co-ordinated and integrated services than others. In general, institutional arrangements where primary care providers operate in solo practices and are paid for on a fee-for service basis may be the least conducive to meeting new chronic care needs. This partly reflects the fact that, in many systems, doctors are not be remunerated for services of counselling, education and guidance. This contrasts with, for example, the approach in England where there is a progressive move to multi-doctor practices running practice teams, providing scope for a wider range of services that are better adapted to meeting patient needs on a co-ordinated basis. Similarly, the American chronic care model or the advanced medical home concepts are specifically focused on reorganising and reorienting physician practice towards systematic efforts to improve quality of care for the chronically ill (Bodenheimer *et al.*, 2002; Wagner *et al.*, 2001; American College of Physicians, 2006).

The performance of these models will strongly depend on contractual relations between the providers and payers. Contracts need to be widened to specifically include services that enhance care co-ordination and payment arrangements should be adjusted to align incentives appropriately. In particular, so-called soft skills relating to counselling and guidance need to be acquired and remunerated. The analysis of questionnaire replies suggests that perceived problems of care co-ordination are possibly less marked in countries that use mixed payment systems, suggesting that countries use other methods may need to modify the contractual terms of current remuneration schemes to encourage the willingness and capacity of professionals to provide co-ordinated service delivery.

Selective contracting by the primary caregiver with other providers is another way to enhance care co-ordination through alternative remuneration arrangements. The extension of the purchasing role of primary care physicians to a wide range of services in the United Kingdom provides the primary care doctor with greater capacity to ensure access to care and oversee care episodes.[11] It also ensures that the practice reaps a large part of the financial benefits from good oversight of patients; for example, they benefit directly from lower unplanned hospital stays. However, for this to work, the number of available providers must be large enough to make the health care market contestable. Such systems will also need to guard against under-spending or ignoring patients needs and preferences by physicians (Dusheiko *et al.,* 2007).

Care co-ordination may benefit from greater health-system integration

The survey found that care co-ordination problems are the most difficult at the interfaces between health care sectors and between providers. This suggests, in turn, that co-ordination can be improved by a better bridging of administrative and other barriers that impede easy transitions from one sector or provider to another. This issue may be particularly important for transitions into long-term care. Long-term care is often the responsibility of local governments while oversight of the health care system is at state/region or national levels. This can lead to a focus on maximising budgets for individual sectors or institutions (*e.g.*, attempts to shift costs onto other budgets) rather than on evaluating how overall health-care systems can provide care most efficiently and effectively. Such situations also make it more difficult to achieve patient-centred care and better clinical integration. Policy makers could focus on better integration in the area of long-term care, where medical and social care are often intimately linked. Pooling resources between the health and social sectors for designated care co-ordinators who help patients and families at these transition points may be one model to bridge administrative barriers. Integration has the potential to transform complex and fragmented systems of health and social care to make them more "patient-friendly". In practice, countries have many different approaches to achieving greater integration involving many other health care professionals than doctors (Leichsenring, *et al.*, 2004).

In the United States, some of the large HMOs appear to be successful in providing better-co-ordinated care for the chronically ill, something that is probably facilitated by the provision of integrated care within a single organisation. A wide range of collaborative, but less integrated, arrangements between providers are also emerging, but they are only partly aimed at better clinical integration (*e.g.* Integrated Care Organisation – ICOs) (Mechanic, 2004). The introduction of integrated care contracts in Germany is increasing incentives to improve active purchasing across health care settings. Primary care clinics such as those in Spain and some of the Nordic countries are also better adapted to providing co-ordinated-care services, while the re-emergence of polyclinics in Germany and the networking models in France (known as *réseaux et filières*) provide examples of other alternatives.

Creating the conditions for better clinical integration is particularly important and requires careful attention. Reform programmes need to ensure that care integration is not blocked by professional resistance that may be linked, for example, to lack of mutual esteem and recognition between providers at the primary and long-term care levels. Attention also needs to be given to the effects of possible interactions between payment arrangements across different sectors, for example where prospective case-based payments lead to increased (unnecessary) hospital activity even if there is capacity to provide this service more cost effectively in the ambulatory care sector. Such problems could be tackled by giving the ambulatory care providers a stronger role of oversight in the system, perhaps by giving them, as suggested above, a stronger purchasing function for care from outside the practice. The pooling of resources between the health and social sectors for specific tasks could also be considered – for example for staff, such as care co-ordinators, case managers or transition managers who can help co-ordinate care and act as a bridge between sectors (Coleman, 2003).

Conclusions

In sum, there is scope for improving performance in co-ordination by changing existing health care systems through a policy mix ranging from better organised ambulatory care to patient-centred integration of health and long-term care. While the suggested areas for policy reflection are not new, they may now have greater policy relevance as the importance of chronic disease increases. There are a number of reform areas which may help make health care systems more responsive to new needs but will require closer examination in the future. Countries have already begun to respond. The form of these policies has often reflected the particular difficulties and institutions specific to individual countries.

Disease or case management programmes are one approach to improving care co-ordination. These policies appear to provide scope for improving quality of care, although their capacity to achieve cost savings remains unclear. This may reflect the fact that, in many cases, programmes have not been followed over long enough periods. Better evaluation is needed about which policies appear to work best and in which set of circumstances.

More comprehensive efforts to improve care co-ordination require a mix of policies that go beyond disease management. Care management at transitions to long-term care or better integration of care within individual institutions are two of the many possible examples. These approaches need to address the continuing issue of fragmentation of health care delivery and require payers and providers across care sectors to engage in making care more patient-centred with a focus on multi-disciplinary care. For this to happen, better models of care delivery and payment schemes may need to be devised and evaluated. Progress in assessing the impact of policies also requires better oversight by payers backed up by information systems and regular reporting so as to enhance the scope for programme evaluation.

Notes

1. The impact of ageing on chronic disease and on health- and long-term care expenditure will, nonetheless, depend on a range of factors incuding. improvements in the quality and, effectiveness of care (Oliveira Martens and de la Maisonneuve, 2006; Joyce et al., 2005; and Goldman et al., 2005).

2. The importance of chronic disease in overall costs may increase because of epidemiological changes. While alcohol and tobacco consumption has declined in a number of countries, smoking by women and among young people continues to rise. At the same time, the increase in overweight and obese individuals in most OECD countries is notable and is leading to significantly higher risks of circulatory problems, kidney failure, heart disease and, above all, of diabetes (Andreyeva et al. 2007). Rates of diseases related to obesity are rising among youth, and disability rates and chronic diseases are increasing rapidly among lower age groups (International Diabetes Federation, 2006; American Academy of Pediatrics, 2005). This will likely lead to higher rates of chronic conditions during adulthood (Perrin *et al.,* 2007).

3. While almost three countries out of four see a general practitioner managing patients at the interface between primary care providers and ambulatory specialists, the likelihood of guidance from the primary care level declines at successive interfaces such that only one in five countries judged that guidance to patients is given often by a primary care provider.

4. However, 30% of countries indicate that they infrequently refer hospital patients back to primary care providers, suggesting, for example, that problems of information transmission may be important in many countries.

5. In addition, countries that are particularly concerned with problems at these interfaces also appear to be those that are highly concerned about efficiency issues more generally (see Figure 3.2).

6. For example, Boerma (2003) finds that home visits are more likely if providers are paid on a fee-for-service basis and that GPs spend less time with patients in countries where they work under a mixed capitation scheme (compared with countries with salary and fee-for-service arrangements).

7. Germany, England, and the United States were unable to reply to the questionnaire.

8. Better performance was partly attributed to the strong ICT support systems in the last two institutions. In this context, payment-for-performance approaches were also seen as having a positive impact.

9. IGAS also notes that in the United States a number of other factors can reduce the impact of such programmes including: lack of insurance coverage; cultural barriers for ethnic minorities; proximity to care; co-morbidities and mental problems.

10. Although very few patients have exercised this option but it may be appropriate for individuals with a single chronic condition requiring close specialist attention.

11. While the Primary Care Trust holds the budget for health care provision in the geographical area for which it has responsibility, primary care practice can take on the purchasing function on the basis of indicative budgets.

Bibliography

American Academy of Pediatrics (2005), "Care Co-ordination in the Medical Home: Integrating Health and Related Systems of Care for Children with Special Health-Care Needs", *Pediatrics,* Vol. 116, No. 5, pp. 1238-1244.

American College of Physicians (2006), *The Advanced Medical Home: A Patient-Centered, Physician Guided Model for Health Care*, Policy Monograph. Available at *www.acponline.org/hpp/adv_med.pdf*

Andreyeva T. *et al.* (2007), "Obesity and Health in Europeans Aged 50 Years and Older", *Public Health*, Vol. 121, No. 7, pp. 497-509.

Asch, S.M. *et al.* (2006), "Who is at Greatest Risk for Receiving Poor-Quality Health Care?", *New England Journal of Medicine*, Vol. 354, No. 11, pp. 1147-1156.

Bodenheimer, T. *et al.* (2002), "Improving Primary Care for Patients with Chronic Illness", *Journal of the American Medical Association*, Vol. 288, No. 15, pp. 1775-1779.

Boerma, W.G.W. (2003), *Profiles of General Practice in Europe: An International Study of Variation in the Tasks of General Practitioners*, NIVEL, Utrecht.

Coleman, E.A. (2003), "Falling Through the Cracks: Challenges and Opportunities for Improving Transitional Care for Persons with Continuous Complex Care Needs", *Journal of the American Geriatric Society*, Vol. 51, No. 4, pp. 549-555.

Coxon, K. *et al.* (2004), "Inter-professional Working and Integrated Care Organizations", in J. Billings and K. Leichsenring (eds.) *Long-Term Care in Integrating Health and Social Care Services for Older Persons, Evidence from Nine European Countries*, European Centre, Ashgate, Vienna.

Docteur, E. and H. Oxley (2003), "Health Care Systems: Lessons from the Reform Experience", OECD Health Working Papers, No. 9, OECD Publishing, Paris.

Dusheiko, M. *et al.* (2007), "The Impact of Budgets for Gatekeeping Physicians on Patient Satisfaction: Evidence from Fundholding", *Journal of Health Economics*, Vol. 26, No. 4, pp. 742-762.

Goldman, D. *et al.* (2005), "The Value of Elderly Disease Prevention", *Forum for Health Economics and Policy*, Vol. 9, No. 2.

Howe, R. (2005), *The Disease Manager's Handbook*, Jones and Bartlett Publishers, Boston, MA.

IGAS (2006), "Améliorer la prise en charge des malades chronique: les enseignements des expériences étrangères de 'disease management'", Report presented by Pierre Louis Bras, Gilles Duhamel and Etienne Grass, Inspection Générale des Affaires Sociales, Paris.

International Diabetes Federation (2006), *Diabetes Atlas, Third Edition,* International Diabetes Federation, Brussels.

Joyce, G.F. *et al.* (2005), "The Lifetime Burden of Chronic Disease among the Elderly", *Health Affairs*, Vol. 24, Suppl. 2, pp. W5R 18-29.

Kohn, L.T. *et al.* (2000), *To Err is Human: Building a Safer Health System*, National Academy Press, Washington, DC.

Leichsenring, K. *et al.* (2004), "Moments of Truth. An Overview of Pathways to Integration and Better Quality", in J. Billings and K. Leichsenring (eds.), *Long-Term Care in Integrating Health and Social Care Services for Older Persons, Evidence from Nine European Countries*, European Centre, Ashgate, Vienna.

Liljas, B. and A. Lahdensuo (1997), "Is Asthma Self-Management Cost Effective?", *Patient Education and Counseling*, Vol. 32, pp. S97-104.

Mechanic, D. (2004), "The Rise and Fall of Managed Care", *Journal of Health and Social Behaviour*, Vol. 45 (Suppl), pp. 76-86.

Oliveira Martens, M.J. and C. de la Maisonneuve (2006), "The Drivers of Public Expenditure on Health and Long-Term Care: An Integrated Approach", *OECD Economic Studies*, No. 42, OECD Publishing, Paris.

Perrin, J.M. *et al.* (2007), "The Increase of Childhood Chronic Conditions in the United States", *Journal of the American Medical Association*, Vol. 297, No. 24, pp. 2755-2759.

Schoen, C. *et al.* (2005), "Taking the Pulse of Health Care Systems: Experiences of Patients with Health Problems in Six Countries", *Health Affairs*, Suppl Web Exclusives:W5-509-25.

Wagner, E.H. *et al.* (2001), "Improving Chronic Illness Care: Translating Evidence Into Action", *Health Affairs,* Vol. 20, No. 6, pp. 64-78.

Chapter 4.

Ensuring Efficiency in Pharmaceutical Expenditures[1]

By Elizabeth Docteur, formerly Deputy Head of the Health Division,
and Valérie Paris, Health Division, OECD

This chapter examines options for ensuring good value for money in pharmaceutical expenditure, keeping in mind both the short- and the long-term view. It then discusses the scope for improvement to existing policies and emerging alternative approaches.

Introduction

OECD countries collectively spent more than USD 550 billion on pharmaceutical products in 2005, accounting for about 1.5% of gross domestic product (GDP). Although pharmaceutical expenditure accounts for a relatively minor share of OECD countries' spending on health care on average less than a fifth of total health expenditure) the share has been increasing over the past 20 years. Spending on pharmaceuticals is growing at an average rate of 5.7% per year, faster than average growth in expenditure on other types of health care, and faster than GDP.

Policy makers' interest in pharmaceutical expenditure and its growth relative to the economy as a whole reflects the large public stake in financing. The public sector is the primary source of financing for pharmaceuticals, accounting for 60% of total pharmaceutical expenditure in OECD countries, on average. Nevertheless, households generally spend more out of pocket for pharmaceuticals than for other forms of health care. Among 17 countries for which data are available, the average share of out-of-pocket expenditure in total pharmaceutical expenditure in 2005 was 32%, compared to 18% for total health expenditure.

Variation in per capita spending on pharmaceuticals is notable in its relative consistency across OECD countries: half spent within 20% of the average in 2005.[2] The United States spent the most (close to double the OECD average) and Mexico the least (less than half the average).

Differences in per capita expenditure levels reflect differences in the level of retail prices paid for pharmaceutical products and in the volume and mix of products consumed. Five countries (Canada, Iceland, Germany, Switzerland and the United States) had average retail prices that were 30% to 85% above the OECD average. Nine countries (Australia, the Czech Republic, Greece, Hungary, Korea, Poland, the Slovak Republic, Spain, and Turkey) had price levels between 68% and 81% of the OECD average. Differences in retail prices reflect not only differences in prices received by manufacturers for their products but also important differences in distribution costs (ranging from about 20% to 37% of retail prices) and value-added taxes (ranging from 0 to 21% of retail prices).

With the exception of the United States, the countries that consumed the most pharmaceuticals in 2005 (Australia, France and Spain) had below-average retail price levels.[3] Mexico, New Zealand, Poland and the Slovak Republic, had the lowest level of consumption. Income per capita is positively correlated across countries with both the volume of pharmaceutical consumption and expenditure per capita. However, per capita income explains only one quarter of the variability observed in the per capita volume of consumption across OECD countries, and even less of the variability in expenditure or price levels, indicating that other explanatory factors are at work.

Pharmaceutical markets differ notably in the availability and use of generic alternatives to original products that have gone off-patent, and in the extent to which significant savings are achieved through price competition in the off-patent market. Generic products accounted for just 14% of the global market in terms of value, although more than 40% of products sold in several large markets, including Germany, the United Kingdom and the United States, are generics. By contrast, generics have less than a 10% share of the market in terms of both volume and value in Belgium, Italy, Portugal and Spain.

Pharmaceutical policy making can have multiple objectives that must be balanced with one another to arrive at the policy mix that best reflects national priorities. The objective of ensuring affordable access to effective medicines runs up against strong pressures for public cost containment. There is also a tension between health system performance objectives and those pertaining to industry in several OECD countries which have, or aspire to have, a significant domestic pharmaceutical industry presence and activity.

But perhaps the most difficult trade-off in pharmaceutical policy is that between static efficiency (maximising consumer welfare by getting the most health value from today's expenditures constrained by the limits of present technological capability) and dynamic efficiency (creating incentives for research and development of products that improve capacity to prevent health conditions and cure diseases in the future). Getting the best possible price or lowest possible expenditures for pharmaceutical products in the market today may mean having fewer and less innovative alternatives for the future.

This chapter is intended to help policy makers consider options for ensuring good value for money in pharmaceutical expenditure, keeping in mind both the short- and the long-term view. It is important to recognise that the appropriateness of particular policies depends heavily on national context and the weights ascribed to objectives when making trade-offs. The first section provides an overview of current policies and their impact on efficiency of pharmaceutical expenditure, noting key trade-offs with other goals. The second section suggests improvements and points out emerging alternative policies. A policy checklist summarises key considerations for policy makers seeking to enhance efficiency.

Current policies, instruments and experiences and their impact

While each OECD country has a unique mix of pharmaceutical policies, their policy environments share several common features that have important implications for the resulting market dynamics. First, all OECD countries have established systems of intellectual property rights (IPR) designed to foster innovation by providing innovators with rights that exclude unauthorised production and sale of an invention for a set period of time. Second, all have established regulatory authorities that authorise firms to market their products on the condition that they meet standards of quality, safety, and efficacy. Despite some cross-country variations in IPR and marketing authorisation, these types of policies all typically raise prices by limiting the potential for competition.

On the other hand, OECD countries show a great diversity in the coverage of the population against pharmaceutical expenditures, in pricing and reimbursement policies, and in policies used to influence the volume and mix of drugs used.

Coverage of pharmaceuticals

In an effort to promote affordable access to pharmaceuticals, all countries subsidise the purchase of pharmaceuticals for some or all of their populations. OECD governments generally treat pharmaceuticals (like health services generally) as a merit good, that is, a good whose consumption should not be determined solely by individual preferences and ability to pay.[4] Here, there is a great deal of variation among OECD countries, ranging from financing of public clinics that provide pharmaceuticals to the uninsured in Mexico, to the tax subsidies for employer-sponsored health insurance benefits in the United States.

The coverage schemes that subsidise the amount individuals spend on pharmaceuticals and protect them against the risk of incurring high out-of-pocket costs also distort the pharmaceutical market, affecting both prices and volumes of consumption. They define the degree to which the pharmaceutical market is subsidised, with greater subsidies resulting in relatively lower consumer price elasticity of demand. While there is great cross-country variation in cost-sharing requirements, individuals in OECD countries typically bear much less than half the cost of their pharmaceutical consumption. As a result, consumption is greater than it would be if individuals paid the full cost.

Forms of pharmaceutical coverage: from uniform coverage by a single scheme to multiple plans offered by competing providers

Most OECD countries have a common scheme for pharmaceutical coverage: national regulations define the benefits covered (or excluded) and the level of cost sharing, though coverage may be provided by a single scheme or by multiple insurers, competing or not. By contrast, in a few OECD countries (*e.g.*, the United States and Canada), pharmaceutical coverage is mainly supplied by competing insurers, which are free to define premiums, benefits covered, and the level of cost sharing.

This distinction is important in that it largely defines the market power of the payers or purchasers, which is determined by the number of potential customers represented (considered as a share of the total market for a product) and their willingness and ability to pay.[5] Within a country, a system with a single purchaser or authority acting on behalf of payers collectively will have greater power to obtain price concessions from pharmaceutical sellers, compared to a system in which the national market features multiple schemes operating (and purchasing) independently. However, competing insurers or funds may be able to be more active or discriminating in their purchasing efforts to best meet the demands of those covered, to the extent that those persons are free to choose a competitor – including one that is more or less active in purchasing – if they are dissatisfied.

Formularies determine comprehensiveness of pharmaceutical coverage

Coverage schemes vary greatly in the range of benefits offered. In schemes with what are known as open formularies, every prescription drug approved for marketing is covered and the schemes generally act as price takers. Certain categories of medicines may be excluded, or particular products specified on a so-called negative list (as used in Germany and the United Kingdom, for example). Most coverage schemes adopt positive lists or closed formularies which list drugs covered by the scheme and associated restrictions (second course therapy, prescription by a specialist, prior authorisation, limitation of reimbursement to some indications, etc.), as well as the level of reimbursement or cost sharing. The criteria used to determine inclusion in positive lists varies, and may or may not include a formal assessment of the cost-effectiveness of a product relative to therapeutic alternatives.

Coverage restrictions are arguably blunt instruments compared with practice guidelines and other tools at the disposal of policy makers. Even so, they can be used to promote value-for-money in pharmaceutical spending, steering consumption and reimbursement towards the most cost-effective medicines. Furthermore, coverage schemes that are empowered to select some drugs and exclude others within a therapeutic area, or that can grant preferred status for some drugs, benefit from increased purchasing power in price negotiations with pharmaceutical companies.

Cost-sharing mechanisms are used to contain and steer the demand for pharmaceuticals

Most drug coverage schemes in OECD countries require that users contribute to the cost of medicines they consume through prescription fees, co-insurance rates and, more rarely, deductibles. From the payer's point of view, cost-sharing mechanisms shift costs towards users and can steer the demand for pharmaceuticals. Private insurers in the United States use tiered co-payments to orient patients' demand towards the most cost-effective treatments (the cheapest therapeutic alternative). Public schemes less commonly use this option, other than in the case of generic substitution.

The downside of cost sharing is that it risks impairing access and compromising patient compliance with prescribed regimens. Cost sharing has been shown to be effective in reducing demand, although the effects fall disproportionately on people with lower incomes and the chronically ill. Lexchin and Grootendorst (2004) reviewed studies measuring the impact of increases in cost sharing on vulnerable populations (poor, beneficiaries of social assistance, people with chronic diseases and those with poor health status) in OECD countries.[6] Virtually all studies demonstrated that increased cost sharing resulted in reduced use of medicines by low-income people and the chronically ill. Other studies showed that even less vulnerable groups can be affected by cost-sharing requirements, reducing their demand for essential drugs following an increase in co-payments (see, for example, Paris and Docteur, 2006, for a review of Canadian studies and Leibowitz *et al.*, 1985).

Cost-sharing policies can be structured to limit the risk of affordability problems. Many OECD countries make special coverage provisions for those in need, including exemptions and caps on out-of-pocket spending. For example, Sweden uses a graduated cost-sharing mechanism whereby the co-payment diminishes as out-of-pocket payments increase over the course of a year. Total yearly outlays for patients are capped at SEK 1 800 (Moïse and Docteur, 2007b).

Reference pricing, setting common reimbursement amounts for a cluster of drugs, is a practice by which payers seek to get good value for money in pharmaceutical expenditure

Under normal market conditions, informed consumers compare products to determine if added benefits are worth added costs. This is difficult in the case of pharmaceuticals, both because information on relative benefits is not always available at the time of decision making and because patients rely heavily on physicians to act as their agents in choosing appropriate medicines. The practice of setting a common reimbursement amount for similar products, leaving patients to pay the difference out of pocket if they use more expensive alternatives, is somewhat misleadingly known as reference pricing. Reference pricing is attractive in the sense that, theoretically, only those products with advantages valued by patients and their physicians should receive a premium price. In practice, however, manufacturers often prefer to price at the reference point rather than risk losing market share in imperfectly operating markets. In fact, the practice of reference pricing provides incentives for manufacturers to differentiate their products before market entry to the extent necessary to avoid inclusion in an established cluster, so as to achieve a price premium. If the product is not highly innovative, companies may seek to provide evidence of effectiveness for a new indication or for a targeted population.

Many OECD countries define fixed reimbursement amounts for clusters of products. Most often, clusters include only bio-equivalent off-patent products, but a small number of countries (*e.g.*, Germany and the Netherlands) form broader clusters of products which are therapeutically equivalent, including patented drugs.

The net impact of reference price policies in terms of cost-containment is difficult to assess. First, such an assessment requires evidence on costs trends for clustered products. Second, one must also have similar evidence for those which are not clustered in order to capture all potential effects on pharmaceutical expenditure trends. Finally, assessment requires a sound empirical methodology that allows for the disentangling of the effect of the reference price policy from the effects of other concurrent policies and contextual market features, such as generic entry and penetration (Puig-Junoy, 2005). Results from an extensive review undertaken by the Cochrane collaboration showed contrasting results across a number of therapeutic classes (Aaserud *et al.*, 2006).[7]

Pricing policies

Manufacturers can exploit a monopoly position when facing relatively inelastic demand for medicines. Because of this, many countries regulate prices for at least some portion of the pharmaceutical market. Two countries with pluralistic coverage schemes, Canada and Mexico, have established price regulation for on-patent pharmaceuticals to assure that prices paid by any part of the population, insured or not, are not excessive. In most other OECD countries, coverage schemes require manufacturers to accept price limits in exchange for subsidisation through reimbursement schemes, serving as *de facto* regulation for that part of the market covered by reimbursement.[8] Even in the United States, manufacturers must submit to price regulation if they wish to be reimbursed under Medicaid and the Veterans Health Administration, the public schemes providing coverage to 19% and 2.6% of the US population, respectively.

Regulatory authorities use a common set of tools to define or limit the prices charged by pharmaceutical firms. The most common approaches are reviewed below.

External price benchmarking

External benchmarking of pharmaceutical prices in other jurisdictions is the most widely used technique to limit prices and reimbursement in OECD countries. Public authorities use it to assess the appropriateness of the proposed (or actual) price in relation to what is paid elsewhere. External benchmarking requires an explicit or implicit notion about how pharmaceutical prices ought to differ across countries. The reference pricing policies employed by OECD countries reflect different perspectives on these questions. European countries, for example, generally refer to each other, that is, they tend to choose countries with similar economic comparability or geographic proximity. Germany and the United Kingdom (both of which allow free pricing for new drugs at market entry and are often first- or early-launch countries) , together with France, are the three countries most commonly referenced.

The way in which the benchmark prices are used also varies across countries. Most countries set the price level (often a ceiling) as a function of the average price of the benchmarked countries, or subset thereof. In Japan, external benchmarking is used to adjust the price of any new drug, positively or negatively, if it differs significantly from the average of the drug's price in France, Germany, the United Kingdom, and the United States (Inazumi, 2008).

The rationale for selecting particular benchmark countries is not always explicit and thus the effects can be unpredictable. Despite very different contexts, price regulation in both Canada and Switzerland has reduced the gap in prices with the richest European countries, but increased the gap with US prices (Paris and Docteur, 2006; Paris and Docteur, 2007). In Mexico, on the other hand, there may be no impact on prices obtained by manufacturers because the system is loosely regulated and readily gameable (Moïse and Docteur, 2007a).

Widespread benchmarking is problematic. First, it provides manufacturers with incentives to launch first in countries that do not regulate pharmaceutical prices at market entry and with relatively low price elasticity of demand, in order to have the list prices in these countries referenced by others. Second, the use of confidential agreements between manufacturers and purchasers in some countries (in which the list price is disconnected from the price actually paid by purchasers) raises questions as to the appropriate price level for benchmarking purposes. If regulators of referencing countries rely on listed prices to make their decisions, they may pay higher prices than they intended. The less transparent the outcome of the negotiation process, the less predictable its impact on referencing countries.

External benchmarking practices may result in premiums for products based on their status as new market entrants, unless benchmarking is combined with considerations of a product's value and cost-effectiveness. Furthermore, it provides firms with incentives to invest in the development of very marginal modifications of existing products (*e.g.,* formulations, dosage) with no benefit to patients in terms of therapeutic effect in order to avoid benchmarking and parallel trade within the European Union.

Internal reference pricing

Internal reference pricing, *i.e.* pricing drugs by reference to therapeutic comparators, is used by some payers and regulators at market entry. The therapeutic advantages of a new drug are compared with existing competitors; regulators generally agree to grant a higher price to drugs with demonstrated therapeutic advantages. In principle, internal price referencing replicates what would happen in a well-functioning market in which well-informed consumers would accept higher prices for new goods only if these were utility-enhancing relative to alternatives. However, regulators have different views about what should be considered as a therapeutic advantage and are more or less inclined to grant premiums to products presenting incremental improvements.

At least four OECD countries (Canada, France, Japan, and Switzerland) consider the prices of similar products already on the market as a guide to pricing new products with therapeutic comparators. In each country, products that are considered therapeutically superior can be priced at a premium compared to therapeutic alternatives. In Canada, the Patented Medicine Prices Review Board classifies new patented entrants in one of three categories, according to the level of novelty of the new product. Only the most innovative products are granted a premium for innovation. Japan, France, and Switzerland also consider the degree of new entrants' innovativeness for the purpose of negotiating the prices of new drugs being considered for addition to the positive list.

Generic price linkage is a specific form of internal reference pricing used by several OECD countries. In those cases, the generic is priced at market entry at a discount relative to the price of the original product. For instance, generic drugs must be priced at least 50% below the price of the off-patent original in France, and in Switzerland, at least 30% below.

Promoting the greatest value in pharmaceutical expenditure requires that referenced products are priced to reflect their value. This may not always be the case in countries relying on external benchmarking to set prices for products that are first entrants in a therapeutic class. Beyond this, internal referencing still requires decisions as to which variations warrant paying more and how much more.

The impact of internal reference pricing on profits and research and development (R&D) incentives depend on the willingness of payers to recognise incremental innovation and to pay for it. Such policies may influence late stages of the R&D process, in which firms try to discover new applications for their products in order to differentiate them from potential competitors and obtain price premiums. This does not necessarily lead to more new products but to more applications, formulations, or other line extensions.

Pricing based on pharmaco-economic assessment

Cost-effectiveness analysis and other methods of pharmaco-economic assessment are used to put in perspective the incremental cost of a medicine with its incremental benefit in terms of relevant health outcomes.[9] Formal cost-effectiveness studies can be used in two ways to determine whether a product will be reimbursed or subsidised and at which price:

- When therapeutic alternatives are available, incremental cost-effectiveness is usually used to make decisions as to whether the new product can be considered worth the additional cost.

- When no therapeutic alternative is available, an implicit or explicit definition of a cost-effectiveness threshold is required (Eichler *et al.*, 2004).

Cost-effectiveness is generally not assessed for pricing but rather to decide whether or not a product should be reimbursed at the price proposed by the manufacturer. Several OECD countries now undertake pharmaco-economic assessments, or closely review the assessments provided by pharmaceutical firms, in the course of coverage and pricing decisions. However, it is very difficult to assess the degree to which countries make effective use of pharmaco-economic assessment (Dickson *et al.*, 2003; Drummond *et al.*, 2003).

Pharmaco-economic assessment may be produced systematically or on a case by case basis. For instance, cost-effectiveness analysis is undertaken systematically for every new drug in Australia and Sweden, and for every new compound in Canada. By contrast, the National Institute of Clinical Excellence (NICE) in England and Wales uses pharmaco-economic assessment upon request, to recommend whether or not the National Health Service (NHS) should subsidise certain medicines, with the main objective of avoiding exclusion of those products from the formularies of primary care trusts.

Countries vary in how they evaluate costs and outcomes. For instance, in Sweden, costs and benefits are considered from a social perspective, rather than from the perspective of the payer, which is rather singular among OECD countries. The social perspective can be at odds with responsibilities and objectives of decision makers in charge of ensuring efficient use of resources allocated to the health system, however (Brouwer *et al.*, 2006). Interventions deemed cost-effective at the societal level may well be costly and not cost-effective for the payer. OECD countries more typically use the payer perspective.

Another difference in the assessment of clinical outcomes is the extent to which surrogate endpoints (*e.g.* tumour shrinkage) are considered to be valuable outcomes, or whether the payer instead requires evidence of improvements in health and disability status. Decision-makers must also decide on how to proceed in the face of uncertainty about efficacy. The uncertain reliability of information submitted by pharmaceutical firms, including clinical and economic claims, present problems for decision makers. A study of decisions made by the Australian Pharmacy Benefits Advisory Commission showed that the probability of acceptance of a technology was higher – cost-effectiveness being constant – when the level of confidence in clinical claims was higher (Harris *et al.*, 2006).

Assessment may be used to compare therapeutic alternatives within a therapeutic area or to compare the cost-effectiveness of health interventions across the health system as a whole. The latter approach supposes the definition of cost-effectiveness thresholds, in terms of cost per "quality adjusted life year" for instance, beyond which the health intervention – or pharmaceutical – will not be subsidised. Policy makers have been reluctant to define such thresholds explicitly; instead seeming to employ one or more implicit thresholds and to ignore them in special circumstances, as sometimes is the case for orphan drugs or for drugs treating life-threatening diseases for which no alternative treatment is yet available (Eichler *et al.*, 2004).

In addition, there is the question of how cost-effectiveness thresholds should be set to recognise citizens' willingness to pay for drugs. The World Health Organisation (2002) has suggested that a cost-effectiveness threshold equal to three times the GDP per capita per DALY (disability adjusted life year) could be a cut-off point for financing health interventions, suggesting that income is the main determinant of citizens' willingness to pay. Some countries or schemes (for example several public plans in Canada) do not adopt official thresholds, but explicitly consider budget constraints in their assessment to decide whether the new treatment is affordable or not, given other priorities.

Finally, pharmaco-economic assessments can yield different results, depending on their focus. NICE assessments generally consider a class of products or different interventions, while other assessment bodies consider isolated products (Sweden) or even a product's indications separately (Canada and Australia). Most often, regulators and payers respond to evidence that products are less cost-effective for certain indications by restricting listing of the product to cost-effective uses, rather than establishing distinct prices.[10]

OECD countries face a number of challenges in the exercise of pharmaco-economic assessment. First, its practice requires a multidisciplinary approach encompassing economics, pharmacology, epidemiology, biostatistics, and medicine. Smaller or lower-income countries may not have enough skilled scientists to carry out systematic pharmaco-economic assessments. For example, in both Mexico and the Slovak Republic, pharmaco-economic evaluations are one of several criteria assessed for reimbursement purposes by the respective authorities, yet there are clear shortfalls in the resources for properly evaluating these (Moïse and Docteur, 2007; Kaló *et al.*, 2008).

Given fixed budget constraints, adoption of new and costly technologies (either high priced or with large population targets) are likely to divert health funds from other interventions that could be more cost-effective. In order to avoid such distortions in fund allocations, the governments in England and Wales decided in 2002 that any positive recommendations of NICE should be allocated supplementary funds to allow local providers to purchase the new technology. Although any new technology approved is thus supposed to lead to supplemental funding, NHS authorities may incorporate future expected decisions in their annual budgetary exercise.

Pharmaco-economic studies are generally considered untransferable across countries because of differences in health care costs and epidemiological contexts. Therefore, one country's use of pharmaco-economic assessment should not be expected to have any direct implications for the price or availability of medicines elsewhere. On the other hand, widespread use of pharmaco-economic assessment in pricing would foster price divergence, reflecting country differences. Yet, if countries consider each other pharmaco-economic studies, one would expect some influence on price convergence. Beyond this, some information resulting from pharmaco-economic studies is likely to be generalisable and transferable.[11]

Subject to the constraints of scientific progress, pharmaceutical R&D will target the types of conditions for which new therapies are rewarded by highest profits. The focus of recent innovations on life-style and minor conditions rather than on those that are life-threatening or disabling suggests that these are more profitable, given the level of R&D investment required in comparison with the returns on investment. Thus, current pricing and purchasing methods are either failing to take therapeutic value adequately into account, or societies have a greater willingness to pay for treatments for minor conditions. By differentiating prices or payments based on product value, pharmaco-economic assessment should encourage investment in more valuable innovations.

Price-volume agreements

As payers seek to minimise the trade-offs required by cost containment measures, they are increasingly experimenting with alternative approaches to purchasing and payment. Price-volume agreements, which focus more directly on achieving the desired level of expenditure on pharmaceuticals, are one such policy.

Given the low marginal cost of production, pharmaceutical firms may be willing to negotiate based on the total value of sales, rather than on a per-unit price basis. This would offer lower-income countries affordable access to medicines without potentially compromising the value of manufacturers' sales elsewhere. However, the policy must be designed to ensure that products are not diverted to other markets.

Payers and purchasers, public or private, may make price-volume agreements at a product level in order to obtain price reductions when volume increases. The discounts and rebates on list prices consented to by manufacturers as part of product-specific price-volume agreements with purchasers or regulators are generally not known, since these agreements are most often confidential. The French authorities, for example, sometimes enter into agreements for products with high sales potential, with the price reduction taking the form of rebates, paid at the end of the year by the manufacturer with no consequences for the listed price. These rebates amounted to 0.94% of French companies' turnover in recent years but are highly concentrated on a few products and firms (Cour des Comptes, 2004; Comité économique des produits de santé, 2007).

Evidence from the United States suggests that these discounts can be substantial, at least for some products. The US Federal Trade Commission (US FTC, 2005) obtained confidential information on contracts between a sample of pharmaceutical benefit management companies (PBMs) (including some of the largest) and 11 large pharmaceutical companies. It used these data to estimate the discounts granted by PBMs to plan sponsors on average wholesale prices in 2003. For brand-name drugs, discounts ranged from 16% to 27.9% of sales in contracts with less restrictive or open formularies, with larger discounts in contracts with more restrictive formularies (US FTC, 2005). In total, the FTC study revealed that manufacturers consented to rebates, on average, of USD 6.34 per brand prescription for inclusion of their drugs in PBMs' formularies, 71% of which were concentrated on the top 25 brand name drugs.

Due to the increasing globalisation of the pharmaceutical industry, manufacturers view the confidential nature of price-volume agreements to be critical to their ability to segment markets for purposes of price differentiation. Even so, based on recent initiatives that facilitate information sharing in Europe and for developing countries, the trend appears to be towards greater transparency in official list prices. This creates a genuine risk of reduced availability in countries where markets cannot sustain top prices. Pharmaceutical firms may choose not to launch in these countries if they cannot negotiate high list prices with confidential discounts. In the public sector, decision makers may face a trade-off between transparency and ability to engage in value-based decision making on pharmaceuticals.

Risk-sharing arrangements

Health insurers and public plans seek to obtain maximum health benefits from their drug purchases. Yet often, reliable information on the outcomes of a product in general use is unavailable at the time of decision making. For this reason, a so-called outcome guarantee, or risk-sharing scheme, may be attractive, particularly when outcomes are in question or the product has a prospectively large cost impact. Under a risk-sharing arrangement, a pharmaceutical company and coverage decision makers agree on the expected outcomes from a drug for a given indication. If the drug fails to fulfil these expectations, the pharmaceutical companies will (partly) refund the health service for the costs (Chapman *et al.*, 2004). Reducing the risk associated with decision making makes it easier for patients and their doctors to try expensive medicines and for manufacturers to sell their products.

One of the most well-known examples of risk-sharing agreements is the scheme for multiple sclerosis drugs in the United Kingdom. Since May 2002, the NHS has paid for four multiple sclerosis products (Avonex, Betaferon, Copaxone, and Rebif) under an agreement made after these treatments were not recommended for use on the basis of cost-effectiveness grounds by NICE (National Institute of Clinical Excellence). The price of the drugs varies according to evidence regarding its effectiveness derived from patients participating in the scheme. If actual outcomes do not meet expectations, within a margin of tolerance, the company must lower the price of the product – which is about USD 20 000 a year per patient. Risk-sharing schemes have only rarely been used and overall results are not publicly available. In any case, periodic reviews of assessments are highly desirable since effectiveness in real use has sometimes proved to be different than claimed efficacy.

Other approaches used to influence demand and mix of pharmaceuticals

Governments and insurers may seek to influence the volume and mix of pharmaceuticals consumed for a variety of reasons, ranging from cost control to quality improvement, although policy makers in most OECD countries have focused more on prices than on other considerations. Coverage schemes differ significantly in how they seek to manage the volume and mix of pharmaceutical consumption; many schemes have few restrictions on choice by physicians and patients while others are active in efforts to affect physician, pharmacist or patient decision making.

Policies geared towards physicians

OECD countries use quite different approaches to influence the prescribing patterns of physicians. In some countries, self-regulation of the medical profession is the standard and initiatives to enhance prescription patterns are led by physicians and pharmacists, focus on quality and clinical effectiveness, and rest on continuing education, quality circles, peer review, and feedback (*e.g.* Switzerland).

In other countries, public authorities or health insurers have imposed or negotiated measures to improve quality or efficiency of prescribing practices. These measures include producing and diffusing clinical guidelines, with voluntary or mandatory compliance, as well as prescription monitoring and feedback. The success of these initiatives is often tied to some type of financial incentive. For example, the success of Sweden's Drug and Therapeutic Committees, which try to change physician prescribing patterns at the local level, have been limited to cases where compliance with recommendations is in conjunction with financial incentives (Moïse and Docteur, 2007).

Some countries have used prescribing budgets in an attempt to control rising drug expenditures. Germany introduced collective prescribing budgets in 1993 for all general practitioners in a district. A collective penalty was applied if the budget was overspent. Although the number of prescriptions decreased, there was concern that this may have compromised the quality of care. The system eventually changed to individual prescription targets in 2001, which were, in turn, based upon regional budgets (Paris and Docteur, 2008). The effect of this new system, with soft, rather than hard, targets is disputed, based upon evidence from the United Kingdom (Walley and Mossialos, 2004) and the Slovak Republic (Kaló *et al.*, 2008).

Policies directed towards pharmacists

Payment for pharmacy services is an important feature of pharmaceutical policies. Most OECD countries continue to link the remuneration of those services to ex-manufacturer prices through mark-ups, often regressive ones. Only a few countries disconnect pharmacists' payments from drug prices, instead using fee schedules defining payment for different tasks of the pharmacist (such as dispensing and patient education).

Many countries have tried to increase the use of generics through policies that allow pharmacists to substitute a generic drug for the prescribed medicine. Most countries that permit generic substitution allow physicians to avert substitution by specifying that the prescription should be dispensed as written. Many also give the patient the right to refuse the substitution, sometimes with the patient paying some or all of the cost difference. Such is the case in Sweden, where generic substitution of the lowest-cost substitutable product (generic or parallel import) is mandatory, and frequent price reductions are possible. The policy seems to have been effective in generating price competition in the off-patent market and in increasing the market share of generics, and has reduced the average level of co-payments for prescribed medicines (Moïse and Docteur, 2007).

Improving policies

Reform or enhance reimbursement and pricing policies to ensure value for money

External and internal price referencing, the tools most widely used by OECD countries to arrive at prices for pharmaceuticals, are problematic in a number of respects. Prices derived through external benchmarking practices are unlikely to accurately reflect the product's value to consumers (in terms of the health improvements, consumer convenience, and other benefits) in the country undertaking the referencing, given the practice of referencing to early-launch or high-sales countries over ones that are similar in terms of income, price level, health costs and health status. The practice of agreeing to confidential rebates that create a gap between the public list price and the actual price paid heightens this problem.

Therapeutic price referencing (or internal referencing) is better in this respect because it explicitly considers whether the added benefits from a new product are worth the added expenditure. Policies that limit reimbursement of similar products to a common level provide pharmaceutical firms with incentives to invest in differentiation of products to avoid inclusion in an existing group, but risk failing to reward incremental innovations when consumers lack information needed to assess value. With respect to innovation, the most problematic scenario is therapeutic referencing that does not allow manufacturers to price above therapeutic competitors, even when the product offers some improvement. Avoiding such potential distortions provides a rationale for policy makers to limit their interventions in the market to the definition of reimbursement levels or public purchase prices, while allowing pharmaceutical firms the freedom to define their sales prices. Under this approach, other policies may be needed to ensure equitable and affordable access to high-cost medicines.

Pharmaceutical reimbursement and pricing policies would be most enhanced by more intensive use of pharmaco-economic assessment as well as agreements linking prices to volumes of sales or to clinical effectiveness.

Increase the role of pharmaco-economic assessment

Efforts to link the level of expenditure for a given pharmaceutical to the value of the benefits offered by the new product – using tools such as pharmaco-economic assessment – are promising for several reasons. First, they can aid in negotiating payments based on considerations of a product's ability to deliver desired outcomes. Policy makers need to ensure, however, that increased efficiency of pharmaceutical expenditure does not come at the expense of efficiency of expenditure in the health sector more broadly. Ideally, pharmaco-economic assessment would be employed in a broader scheme of health technology assessment to make value considerations explicit in health expenditure decision making across the board, rather than for only one type of care.

Second, pharmaco-economic assessment should promote the right level and type of R&D investment, by giving better signals to industry as to which innovations are most highly valued. It can also be used as a tool to establish market-based incentives for investment in treatments for rare conditions.

Because the economic value of the therapeutic benefits (net of costs or savings associated with the use of a product) will vary across countries according to their income, health care costs, epidemiology, and other factors, new pharmaceutical products will have different values in different countries. Thus, adoption of pharmaco-economic evaluation on a widespread basis should result in national expenditures for innovative products differing based on income. At the same time, a move to value-based payment may well result in increased expenditures for certain types of pharmaceutical products in certain countries.

Pharmaco-economic assessment, as with health-technology assessment more generally, is a technically challenging and value-laden exercise. Nevertheless, the perceived value of making an explicit consideration of costs and benefits in price and reimbursement decision making has led about a third of OECD countries to move forward in this area, and several have developed programmes that can provide models for further advances.

Finally, pharmaco-economic assessment addresses one of the most common shortcomings of pharmaceutical pricing and reimbursement policies: the failure to make an explicit assessment of the benefits or expected benefits from a medicine and to use that assessment as a guide to willingness to pay for (or subsidise) new products, taking into account optimal use of the product among the population. Because such assessments link the level of expenditure for a given pharmaceutical product to the value of the benefits offered by the new product, their results can be used by manufacturers to assess willingness to pay for future innovations and should thus provide incentives for development of innovations with the greatest value to patients and society. To the extent that pharmaceutical producers profit more from innovations that have the greatest value to patients and society, they will face incentives to invest more in R&D to produce such therapies.

That being said, pricing and reimbursement policies based on pharmaco-economic assessment can be improved. First, while defining cost-effectiveness thresholds could help to steer innovation towards valued innovation, to date, purchasers have been reluctant to adopt them in a public manner. While clearly such thresholds raise many ethical issues, they could be used by firms to estimate a range of expected returns on investments, according to different levels of effectiveness, price, and volume (Vernon *et al.*, 2005). On the other hand, such thresholds may encourage firms to propose prices higher than they would do absent regulation as long as the threshold is not exceeded. This is a potential problem from a static efficiency perspective, but not necessarily so from the perspective of dynamic efficiency since such price premia may be desirable as a reward for valuable innovation.

Second, using a single cost-effectiveness threshold is problematic because it fails to distinguish among different types of conditions for which therapies may be more highly valued. The approach taken by Sweden is interesting in that multiple implicit thresholds are employed, allowing products to treat conditions for which need for new therapies is greatest to have higher thresholds (Moïse and Docteur, 2007b). Thus these products can be considered cost-effective at a higher price.

Third, although purchasers generally do not publish their cost-effectiveness thresholds, explicit thresholds may hold some promise as a means of providing incentives for investment in R&D to address orphan diseases. Hollis (2005) states that countries may gain from publishing their willingness to pay for orphan drugs as a way to encourage development by defraying the risk of investment.

Finally, there are practical considerations with regards to the systematic implementation of pharmaco-economic assessment in the pricing and reimbursement process. First, as discussed above, it may prove difficult for smaller, lower-income countries to implement. These countries could take advantage of pharmaco-economic assessments done in other countries, revising the inputs to reflect national circumstances. The further development of projects like EURONHEED (a European network of health economic evaluation databases) could help. Second, countries that implement systematic pharmaco-economic assessments need to consider the trade-off between assessments based on objective information and the cost of doing them in-house. Asking manufacturers to submit the results of pharmaco-economic assessments (as is done in Sweden, for example) is less costly (and may be the most realistic alternative in some countries) but may result in assessments that overestimate a product's cost-effectiveness. To a certain extent this risk can be attenuated with vigorous scrutiny of submitted assessments.

Increase the use of volume-price agreements and assess the potential of risk-sharing agreements

Price-volume agreements and risk-sharing agreements represent another interesting development in pricing policy. These practices are attractive in that they focus on benefits obtained for a given level of expenditure rather than on unit price. This is consistent with the perspective of policy makers, who are concerned about the level of total expenditures and the value for money attained, and with reducing the risk associated with decision making when there is uncertainty as to either the size of the prospective market or the outcomes to be expected. It is also consistent with the interests of pharmaceutical firms who care about the return on investment achieved through sales revenues, a function of both price and volume. Thus, an environment in which all those who could potentially benefit from use of a drug had affordable access could be a win-win outcome for both parties.

Nevertheless, it should be noted that not all OECD countries are in a position to take full advantage of price-volume agreements at present. Reimbursement policy in a number of countries stipulates that *all* products in a therapeutic class that are approved for market must be reimbursed. This is justified as a means of providing equal access to the market for pharmaceutical firms, but may in some cases limit the scope for use of coverage restrictions that prefer one drug to another.

Steer demand for pharmaceutical products towards products offering the greatest value

Formulary management can help to steer prescription and demand for pharmaceuticals towards the most cost-effective drugs

Pharmaceuticals obtain market authorisation when there is evidence that they are more effective than a placebo and that their benefit/risk ratio is positive. Head-to-head clinical trials are not required. By contrast, more and more coverage schemes include some form of assessment of therapeutic improvements over competitors as input to the decision as to whether the drug should be reimbursed and at what price. In that regard, positive lists and closed formularies offer better opportunities than negative lists.

Coverage restrictions (such as limited to some indications, second step therapy, subject to prior authorisation) have shown to be effective tools to steer the demand for pharmaceuticals in some contexts (for instance, in public plans in Canada). However, they restrict patient and physician choice in a way that can be unpopular. Having a well-established system for considering exceptional circumstances can help, although this can also impose a cost.

Finally, formulary management may include financial incentives to increase generic use, notably by tiered co-payments or through the setting of fixed reimbursement amounts for therapeutic alternatives. This latest solution appears to be the most efficient, since it caps the payer's expenditures without reducing patients' choice, at least for those patients who are willing and able to pay supplements.

A range of policies can be used to obtain savings when products go off-patent

Generic uptake can also be encouraged through financial incentives for pharmacists. Policy makers should ensure that pharmacists do not earn less when they dispense generics as typically happens when mark-up are defined as a percentage of the ex-factory price. Coverage schemes can encourage generic dispensing either by a specific payment for substitution services or by a specific mark-up. In addition, solutions to enhance generic competition should be tested. The evidence suggests that countries which do not regulate generic prices could have lower prices than regulating countries. Making substitution mandatory is another solution to promote generic use. However, it presents the drawback of reducing choice for patients.

Ensure a more efficient distribution chain

Some of the large differences in distribution costs across OECD countries can be explained by the stringency of the law. For instance, some countries requires wholesalers to supply the full range of available products and expect pharmacists to deliver all products with lengthy open hours, while other countries do not see the need to take this step to ensure accessibility. However, these requirements may not fully explain differences in distribution costs. For example, heavy regulation of pharmacists' services may hamper competition between pharmacists.

Conclusions

Improvement in meeting the multiple objectives of pharmaceutical policy may well be possible without sacrificing cost control. Efforts to improve value for money in public spending on pharmaceuticals could free up resources that could be better spent enhancing the availability, accessibility, and appropriate use of effective medicines. As noted above, many OECD countries could get better value for their money by maximising the use of generic alternatives to off-patent original products, fostering generic price erosion through competition, ensuring efficient distribution systems for prescription and over-the-counter products, and becoming more sophisticated in their reimbursement pricing strategies. Box 4.1 provides a checklist of potential policies for considerations, although these will not necessarily be appropriate for all countries.

Box 4.1. Pharmaceutical policy checklist

Policy makers seeking to increase efficiency in their pharmaceutical expenditures should consult the following checklist to consider:

- obtaining value for money while promoting future innovation by considering relative cost-effectiveness in pricing and purchasing decisions, while ensuring that rewards to innovation are consist with the value of benefits offered.
- seeking opportunities for establishing price-volume agreements or confidential rebates when value-based unit prices cannot be established (due to risk of parallel trade, for example).
- exploring the potential for risk-sharing arrangements to reduce the financial risk presented by new medicines when information on costs and effects is insufficient.
- encouraging generic substitution and price competition in the off-patent market.
- creating incentives for physicians, pharmacists and patients to promote the appropriate prescribing, dispensing and use of medicines, recognising that expenditure includes volume/mix as well as price components.
- considering whether there are opportunities for efficiencies in the distribution chain.
- ensuring that overall health care spending efficiency is not compromised by efforts to improve efficiency of pharmaceutical expenditure.

At present, the lack of a firm foundation and framework for pharmaceutical pricing policy in many OECD countries is reflected in an eclectic mix of policies being employed in ways that are often internally inconsistent. For example, establishing reimbursement mechanisms for pharmacies that link fees to product prices is inconsistent with measures to encourage substitution of lower-priced generic products when these are available. Similarly, the practice of encouraging parallel imports of on-patent products to obtain the lowest possible price diminishes the innovation incentive embedded in the price differential, which is hard to reconcile with practices seeking to establish value-based prices within the country.

Policy makers need to be aware that they do not miss the forest for the trees in their drive to increase efficiency in pharmaceutical expenditure.

Promoting the use of the most cost-effective drug does not increase overall health care spending efficiency if it displaces more cost-effective non-pharmaceutical alternative therapies. Achieving efficiencies in health spending overall should be the objective; efficiencies in pharmaceutical expenditure should be a means to that end.

Notes

1. This chapter draws heavily on analysis presented in *Pharmaceutical Pricing Policy in a Global Market* (OECD, 2008), a report authored by the authors of the present article and by their former colleague Pierre Moïse.

2. This estimate is made by converting expenditures to a common currency and adjusting for differences in economy-wide purchasing power.

3. By adjusting pharmaceutical expenditures for cross-country differences in retail pharmaceutical prices, pharmaceutical consumption levels can be assessed.

4. Need, as proxied by health status measurement, is a typical standard by which an individual's pharmaceutical consumption is assessed.

5. Several US purchasers of pharmaceuticals have more market power than do many universal coverage schemes in OECD countries, when measured in terms of population covered and income. For instance, the population covered by the Veterans' Health Administration exceeds the population of one-third of OECD countries and one pharmaceutical benefits management company, Medco, manages the drug benefit for 60 million people.

6. The review included all studies published in English and French. Of the 24 studies found, all were based in the United States or Canada, with the exception of two studies which were based in Belgium and New Zealand.

7. Of 246 studies reviewed, only two provided reliable estimates of the impact of fixed reimbursement level policies on health plans' drug expenditures. They both analysed the introduction of these schemes in the British Colombia health benefit for seniors.

8. In most countries, manufacturers are free to market their products at any price if the product is not eligible for (or proposed for) reimbursement.

9. Cost-effectiveness analysis is the most commonly used form of pharmaco-economic assessment. Other techniques, such as cost-benefit analysis or cost-utility analysis, might be used under certain circumstances (Dickson *et al.*, 2003).

10. One could imagine a solution for variable pricing if the manufacturer produced different packages for different indications. However, various

actors in the distribution chain would face incentives to substitute a lower-priced equivalent product.

11. Boulenger *et al.* (2005) define generalisability as “the degree to which the results of an observation hold true in other settings” and transferability as “the data, methods and results of a given study are transferable if *a)* potential users can assess their applicability to their setting and *b)* they are applicable to that setting”.

Bibliography

Aaserud, M. *et al.* (2006), "Pharmaceutical Policies: Effects of Reference Pricing, Other Pricing and Purchasing Policies (review)", *The Cochrane Database of Systematic Review*, Vol. 2, Art. No. CD005979.DOI:10.1002/14651858.CD0055979.

Boulenger, S. *et al.* (2005), "Can Economic Evaluations Be Made More Transferable?", *European Journal of Health Economics*, Vol. 6, No. 4, pp. 334-346.

Brouwer, W.B. *et al.* (2006), "A Dollar is a Dollar is a Dollar – Or Is It?", *Value in Health*, Vol. 9, No. 5, pp. 341-347.

Chapman, S., P. Durieux and T. Walley (2004), "Good Prescribing Behaviour", in E. Mossialos, M. Mrazek and T. Walley (eds.), *Regulating Pharmaceuticals in Europe: Striving for Efficiency, Equity and Quality*, Open University Press, Maidenhead.

Comité économique des produits de santé (2007), *Rapport annuel d'activité 2006*, Comité économique des produits de santé, Paris.

Cour des Comptes (2004), *La sécurité sociale*, Cour des Comptes, Paris.

Danzon, P.M. and A. Epstein (2005), "Launch and Pricing Strategies of Pharmaceuticals in Interdependant Markets", Unpublished Working Paper, University of Pennsylvania, 53 pages.

Dickson, M., J. Hurst and S. Jacobzone (2003), "Survey of Pharmacoeconomic Assessment Activity in Eleven Countries", OECD Health Working Papers, No. 4, OECD Publishing, Paris.

Drummond, M.F. *et al.* (2003), "Use of Pharmacoeconomics Information – Report of the ISPOR Task Force on Use of Pharmacoeconomic/Health Economic Evaluation in Health Decision Making", *Value in Health*, Vol. 6, No. 4, pp. 407-416.

Eichler, H.G. *et al.* (2004), "Use of Cost-Effectiveness Analysis in Health-Care Resource Allocation Decision-Making: How are Cost-Effectiveness

Thresholds Expected to Emerge", *Value in Health*, Vol. 7, No. 5, pp. 518-528.

Harris, A.H. *et al.* (2006), "The Determinants of PBAC Recommendations to Fund Drugs in Australia: An Empirical Analysis of the Period 1994-2004", Presentation made at the Medicines Australia and Department of Health and Ageing Policy Conference, Sydney, July.

Hoadley, J. (2005), "Cost Containment Strategies for Prescription Drugs: Assessing the Evidence in the Literature", Report prepared for The Henry J. Kaiser Family Foundation, Washington, DC.

Hollis, A. (2005), *An Efficient Reward System for Pharmaceutical Innovation*, Research Paper, Department of Economics, University of Calgary, Calgary. Available at *http://econ.ucalgary.ca/fac-files/ah/drugprizes.pdf*.

Inazumi, Y. (2008), "Drug Evaluation and Pricing", Presentation by Y. Inazumi, Chief of Drug Price, Economic Affairs Division, Health Policy Bureau, Ministry of Health, Labour and Welfare, Japan, Paris, March.

Kaló, Z., E. Docteur and P. Moïse (2008), "Pharmaceutical Pricing and Reimbursement Policies in Slovakia", OECD Health Working Paper, No. 31, OECD Publishing, Paris.

Knaul, F. *et al.* (2006), "Evidence is Good for Your Health System: Policy Reform to Remedy Catastrophic and Impoverishing Health Spending in Mexico", *The Lancet*, Vol. 368, No. 9549, pp. 1828-1841.

Leibowitz, A., W.G. Manning and J.P. Newhouse (1985), "The Demand for Prescription Drugs as A Function of Cost Sharing", *Social Science and Medicine,* Vol. 21, pp. 1063-1070.

Lexchin, J. and P. Grootendorst (2004), "Effects of Prescription Drug User Fees on Drug and Health Services Use and on Health Status in Vulnerable Populations: A Systematic Review of the Evidence", *International Journal of Health Services*, Vol. 34, No. 1, pp. 101-122.

McMahon, M., S. Morgan and C. Mitton (2006), "The Common Drug Review: A NICE Start for Canada?", *Health Policy*, Vol. 77, No. 3, pp. 339-351.

Moïse, P. and E. Docteur (2007a), "Pharmaceutical Pricing and Reimbursement Policies in Mexico", OECD Health Working Paper, No. 25, OECD Publishing, Paris.

Moïse, P. and E. Docteur (2007b), "Pharmaceutical Pricing and Reimbursement Policies in Sweden", OECD Health Working Paper, No. 29, OECD Publishing, Paris.

OECD (2008), *Pharmaceutical Pricing Policy in a Global Market*, OECD Publishing, Paris.

Paris, V. and E. Docteur (2006), "Pharmaceutical Pricing and Reimbursement Policies in Canada", OECD Health Working Paper, No. 24, OECD Publishing, Paris.

Paris, V. and E. Docteur (2007), "Pharmaceutical Pricing and Reimbursement Policies in Switzerland", OECD Health Working Paper, No. 28, OECD Publishing, Paris.

Paris, V. and E. Docteur (2008), "Pharmaceutical Pricing and Reimbursement Policies in Germany", OECD Health Working Papers, No. 39, OECD Publishing, Paris.

Puig-Junoy, J. (2005), "What is Required to Evaluate the Impact of Pharmaceutical Reference Pricing?", *Applied Health Economics and Health Policy*, Vol. 4, No. 2, pp. 87-98.

Sheldon, T.A. *et al.* (2004), "What's the Evidence that NICE Has Been Implemented? Results from a National Evaluation Using Time Series Analysis, Audit of Patient's Notes, and Interviews", *British Medical Journal*, Vol. 329, pp. 999-1007.

Tamblyn R. *et al.* (2001), "Adverse Events Associated With Prescription Drug Cost-Sharing among Poor and Elderly Persons", *Journal of the American Medical Association*, Vol. 285, No. 4, pp. 421-429.

US Federal Trade Commission (2005), *Pharmacy Benefit Managers: Ownership of Mail-Order Pharmacies*, Federal Trade Commission Report, Washington, DC.

Vernon, J., W.K. Hughen and S.J. Johnson (2005), "Mathematical Modeling and Pharmaceutical Pricing: Analyses Used to Inform In-Licensing and Developmental Go/No-Go Decisions", *Health Care Management Science*, Vol. 8, pp. 167-179.

Walley, T. and E. Mossialos (2004), "Financial Incentives and Prescribing", in E. Mossialos, M. Mrazek and T. Walley (eds.), *Regulating Pharmaceuticals in Europe: Striving for Efficiency, Equity and Quality*, Open University Press, Maidenhead.

World Health Organisation (2002), *World Health Report 2002*, WHO, Geneva.

Chapter 5.

Using ICT to Monitor and Improve Quality in Health Care

By Nicolaas S. Klazinga and Elettra Ronchi
Health Division, OECD

This chapter describes key concepts related to health care quality and information that can be used to measure it. It then considers how current efforts could be furthered by using available technology and examines some important impediments to the wider introduction of ICTs.

Introduction

Strengthening the collection, analysis, sharing and use of health information in order to improve the quality with which medical care is provided has become a policy priority in many OECD countries. In recent years a growing body of empirical evidence has identified significant gaps between how health care should be delivered to achieve the best possible outcomes and how it is delivered in practice (Schuster *et al.*, 1998; Institute of Medicine, 2001; Fisher and Wennberg, 2003; McGlynn *et al.*, 2003). These gaps are so large that a panel of experts convened by the Institute of Medicine (IOM) called it, in a 2001 report, a quality chasm (IOM, 2001).

Although there is controversy regarding the accuracy of available estimates, there is, today, general agreement that quality problems are likely to have a significant health and economic impact in OECD countries. The main sources of such problems are operative errors, generally caused by so-called system failures or wrong decisions. Medication errors alone account for a substantial number of consultations in general practice and hospital admissions across all OECD countries. According to a recently published study (Pirmohamed *et al.*, 2004), the projected annual cost of adverse drug reactions (ADR)-related admissions in the United Kingdom is estimated at GBP 466 million. ADRs are considered to be between the fourth and sixth leading cause of death in the United States (Lazarou *et al.*, 1998).

Medical errors and other deficiencies in the quality of medical care have obvious implications for the performance of health-care systems. Errors, both of omission and of commission, result in harm to the patient and waste financial resources. Policy makers interested in promoting high performance and extracting the maximum value from their health expenditure should, thus, also be interested in designing and maintaining systems that will lead to the fewest number of errors through adherence to established standards for the promotion of high-quality care. Public policies can be put in place that creates incentives for providing care of high quality and to discourage adverse events.

The 2001 IOM report described the lack of co-ordination and communication among providers and between providers and patients as a major cause for the observed quality deficits. It criticised health care systems for their failure to employ electronic information technologies and health care providers for failing both to rely on evidence-based guidelines and to systematically record and report outcomes.

Taken together, the evidence collected over the years and reported in the two IOM publications (IOM, 2000; IOM, 2001) and more recently analysed by the OECD (OECD, 2004) have raised questions as to whether the current model for monitoring and improving health care, based on a fragmented, piece-meal approach towards the collection and use of health information, is still viable. This body of work also calls into question whether the exclusive emphasis on individual responsibility and professional self-regulation, which began with pioneers such as Florence Nightingale and Ernest Codman in the 19th and the early years of the 20th century, is sufficient.

The practice of medicine has changed fundamentally over time. The delivery of care has gradually shifted from individual practitioners to complex, multi-faceted institutions employing a variety of medical and non-medical professionals. Thus, much of care delivery is no longer under the sole control of physicians, let alone one single physician. In light of these changes in medical practice, health-care systems, almost everywhere, are now facing new problems in monitoring health care processes and outcomes. Greater attention is now being paid to the approaches used for quality assurance in medicine, including the specific measures as well as their precision and reliability. It has generated awareness about the need for a more comprehensive and integrated systems approach to collecting health information.

Adoption of information and communication technologies (ICTs) is a critical step for improving health-care quality. Automated data collection and processing can provide rich data in an accessible form that can facilitate benchmarking and be used to identify quality improvement opportunities. A variety of success stories suggest that, when coupled with organisational changes and system re-engineering, measurement-based performance management programmes, investment in information technology, and use of clinical guidelines can make a difference.

The short-term question that arises for policy makers is which policies, institutional, and technical changes for monitoring and improving the quality of care should be implemented. To inform this discussion, this chapter describes several of the strategies that have been implemented in OECD countries. The first section provides a brief explanation of key concepts related to health care quality and the different types of information that can be used for this purpose, their strengths and their weaknesses drawing on the work of the OECD Health Care Quality Indicator Project. The second section considers how current efforts could be furthered by using available technology. The chapter concludes with a review of relevant recent initiatives, an examination of some important impediments to the wider introduction of ICTs, and comments on lessons learnt.

What is quality of care?

While there are many alternatives, the following definition of quality in the health care field from the IOM is widely used: "*Quality is the degree to which health services for individuals and populations increase the likelihood of desired health outcomes and are consistent with current professional knowledge*". This definition assumes that quality is a relative notion and that measuring quality entails finding out whether the processes and outcomes of patient care are consistent with what might be expected or is advised given the available medical scientific and practice knowledge. As this knowledge is, itself, largely based on research conducted on groups of patients, it is, in essence, the application of systematically derived collective information to individuals. Just as work in other scientific fields requires systematic collection and analyses of data, the same holds true for all attempts to measure the quality of health care delivered in medical practice.

Following the parlance in industry, the term quality assessment refers to the neutral process of measurement. Quality assurance refers to combining the measurement with actions to assure a pre-set standard; quality improvement, in turn, refers to those actions where measurement results should lead to performance improvement. Policies associated with these three distinct endeavors can be used to fulfil various functions within health-care systems: promoting accountability of providers towards patients, purchasers and health authorities), improving value in purchasing provider services, increasing patient choice with respect to specific providers, fostering self-improvement by providers, and improving evidence-based decision making. These functions, taken individually, may require different measures to be adapted as not all quality measures are fit for use for all functions.

According to Donabedian (1988), quality is a function of the structure, process, and outcome of care delivery when applied to health care services and to health care systems more broadly, the term quality can also cover aspects such as access, appropriateness, acceptability, timeliness, and continuity of care. In its landmark 2001 report, the IOM also listed efficiency and effectiveness as two of the six main quality aims of a health system (IOM, 2001). Thus, improving quality has an important role to play in increasing the overall efficiency of health care systems. This chapter discusses quality measures in two main dimensions: effectiveness and patient experiences, where measurements of effectiveness are meant to address both the desired health outcomes as well as the potential adverse outcomes, sometimes referred to as safety. Such information should include the content of the care processes and the health outcomes, as well as the notion of time, both in terms of the timeliness with which care is provided and longitudinal measurements (*i.e.,* changes over time). Measurement should also allow assessment of care across settings, and, thus, be both dynamic and unconstrained. These measures should answer key questions, such as whether patients received the full set of services, or only those services, from which they would likely benefit; whether services were provided in a timely and efficient manner; and whether patients benefited from the desired short- and long-term outcomes.

How is quality measured?

There are five major data sources for measuring quality, characterised by increasing degrees of complexity of collection: national registries, administrative data, population surveys, patient surveys and clinical records (Box 5.1). Each of these sources is useful in describing some aspects of quality and some have been used by the OECD in its Health Care Quality Indicators (HCQI) Project.[1] This programme has so far identified 19 cross-country indicators that are reported upon regularly.

Box 5.1. Data sources for measuring quality

Public registries

Public registries for births and deaths. Civil registration is the means by which countries keep track of births, deaths, and marital status of their citizens. Governments require physicians to establish and report deaths to municipal authorities. Burial is often conditional on physician notification. When death registries began documenting causes of death in a systematic way, it became possible to conduct epidemiological studies from recorded mortality data. With international standardisation of causes of death now in place, mortality statistics can be used to monitor causes of death within a country and to compare trends across nations.

Public health registries. Reporting of infectious diseases for public health surveillance is also well established in most countries. Such data can be used to monitor the prevalence and incidence of specific diseases for which there is obligatory reporting by physicians. In combination with birth registries, the data collected can also inform vaccination policies. Birth and health registries are used to plan vaccination schedules in countries with national vaccination programmes.

Disease-specific registries. Disease-specific registries exist but are less frequent. Several countries have cancer registries which have been used as a source for calculating trends in survival rates. Chronic care registries, such as diabetes registers, are more rare and often local or regional. Specialty registries can be found on procedures such as total hip replacement or cardiac bypass graft surgery and related complications.

Administrative databases

Data on demographics, hospital stays, discharge status (alive or not), principal and secondary diagnoses, and procedures are normally included in administrative databases. This administrative data is generally derived from computerised systems used for billing, reimbursement or health care administration (*e.g.* the Uniform Hospital Discharge Set used in the United States). Some databases also contain information from the ambulatory sector on visits, tests, and drugs.

Population surveys

Population surveys are becoming more frequent and are increasingly used to assess quality of care by asking the population about access to care, use of health care services, pharmaceutical consumption, and interpersonal aspects of care delivery, functional outcomes, and symptoms. The World Health Organisation is using population surveys to assess the responsiveness of health systems. The New York-based Commonwealth Fund has been using population surveys to assess specific components of quality of care over the years in various countries, sometimes focusing on specific groups such as the elderly.

Patient surveys

Patient surveys sample persons who recently experienced a specific type of health care in a number of dimensions of care using standardised tools for measurement and reporting. This information is usually accessible from public websites. Although they are available for the broader public, evidence on active use of these data by consumers is scarce. Patient surveys can, however, be important indicators of health system performance and can provide important information on, for example, the functioning of the health care market.

Medical records

The medical record is the systematic documentation over time of a patient's medical history and care, including personal details (name, date of birth, etc.) which are stored locally by a health care provider. Traditionally, medical records have been written on paper and charts and kept in folders. Today, with the advent of information technologies, medical records can be stored electronically and can, in principle, be shared across the continuum of care. The electronic health record is a longitudinal patient record held by various specialists that have been visited by the patient, nursing records and records kept by allied health professionals, including data on tests, procedures and pharmaceutical use. Ideally, it represents a complete patient record that can be assessed at any moment care is delivered, protected by the necessary privacy measures and under control of the patient.

There are two levels of data collection and knowledge construction at work with medical records: at the level of the individual patient and the population level. At the level of the individual patient, the completeness and timeliness of the data are important as well as the assurance that information is stored safely and can be easily retrieved. At the population level, the ideal record should be set up in such a way that information on patients can be traced over time and in various databases for quality assurance purposes, hence the appeal of a unique patient identifier. Doing so requires also standardised coding and recording of procedures, tests, pharmaceutical use, and especially outcomes (health status, functionality status and adverse outcomes). Although some progress has been made in recent years, electronic health records have been very slow to implement.

Table 5.1 groups these indicators based on type of services and by process and outcome. Of these, eleven are derived from national registries (survival rates for colorectal, breast and cervical cancer, asthma mortality rates, incidence and vaccination rates for measles, pertussis, and Hepatitis B) and four are derived from administrative data (case fatality rates for acute myocardial infarction and stroke, hospital admission rate for asthma, waiting times for surgery following hip fractures). Three are partially derived from population surveys (screening rates for breast and cervical cancer and smoking rates), and one (partly) from patient survey data (annual retina exam for diabetic patients).[2]

Table 5.1. Overview of indicators used in the Health Care Quality Indicator Project

Outcome	***Process***
Care for acute conditions	
In-hospital case-fatality rate for acute myocardial infarction	Waiting times for surgery after hip fracture for people aged 65 +
In-hospital case-fatality rate for ischemic and hemorrhagic stroke	
Cancer care	
Survival rate for colorectal cancer	Mammography screening
Survival rate for breast cancer	Cervical cancer screening
Survival rate for cervical cancer	
Care for chronic conditions	
Hospital admission rate for asthma (people aged18+)	Annual retina exam for diabetics
Asthma mortality rate (people aged 5-39)	
Prevention of communicable diseases	
Incidence of measles	Vaccination against measles
Incidence of pertussis	Vaccination against pertussis, diphtheria, and tetanus
Incidence of Hepatitis B	Vaccination against Hepatitis B
	Vaccination against influenza (people aged 65+)
Other	
Smoking rates	

What are the problems for cross-country comparisons?

While generally useful for tracking trends within countries over time, data derived from these sources are less reliable for making comparisons across countries. There are a number of reasons for this. First, differences in the definitions used may make international comparisons problematic, if not impossible. For example, both administrative and register data may not use the same classification systems. Although diagnoses or morbidity data in many countries are based on the International Classification of Diseases (ICD-9 and ICD-10), several countries use the International Classification of Health Interventions (ICHI) and the International Classification of Functioning, Disability and Health (ICF) in a systematic way throughout the health care system. Coding problems are particularly relevant for disease-related registries such as for cancer and diabetes. Although international standardisation of the definitions used in these registries exists, their use is inconsistent and relevant details or information are often missing (for example, staging in cancer diagnoses), thereby limiting their usefulness for constructing comparable adjusted quality indicators. Similarly, not all countries code co-morbidities systematically and comparably in national mortality registries. In this respect, the major shortcomings of administrative databases are due to inaccuracy in coding, lack of specific coding (for example co-morbidities or complications) or lack of information on the severity of the underlying conditions.

Second, in the case of population surveys, there may be problems of inaccuracy with patient self-reporting clinical findings or technical processes (Fowler, 2002). Hence, population surveys may be less precise than data from national registries for specific diseases. For example, screening rates for cancer are estimated in some countries using population surveys where rates could be better documented using data from national screening programmes. Third, patient surveys, like population surveys, suffer from problems of selection and recall bias and the approach used can differ across countries. In the United States, the Consumer Assessment of Healthcare Providers and Systems (CAHPS) approach has been used for measuring patient experiences while the Picker Institute approach has been used in the United Kingdom and some other European countries. In addition, there is concern about the accuracy of patient's reports on clinical findings or technical processes (Fowler, 2002).

Finally, while electronic medical health records provide the most hope for improved assessment of clinical quality in the future, they are still often incomplete. Data is generally available only at an aggregate level and is derived from medical records of groups of patients. They are based on specific diseases, diagnoses (*e.g.* all diabetes patients) or referrals for tests or procedures or medication prescribed (*e.g.* HbA1C levels in diabetes patients, percentage of diabetes patients using insulin) and, most importantly, adverse reactions and other outcomes of care (*e.g.* percentage of diabetes patients developing complications of the eyes, foot or kidneys). Such an approach is based on the assumption that the diagnoses, test results, procedures and outcomes are recorded in a standardised way – which is not always the case.

Improving quality measurement in health care and the role of ICT

Benchmarking can be a useful tool for promoting change and continuous improvement. In particular, cross-national comparisons can help health policy makers determine the causes of shortcomings in the quality of medical care and identify potentially successful responses. Quality measurement still faces formidable challenges, however. Despite the increased availability of measures, problems of comparability and data quality persist. Progress will require changes in the way health information systems are organised and structured and the data collected.

A key challenge involves how to make the most of administrative data. As noted previously, questions about the accuracy and completeness of administrative databases abound because of inconsistency in coding, lack of specificity, and lack of information on the severity of the underlying conditions. Moreover, administrative files contain limited clinical insight to inform quality assessment. They cannot elucidate the interpersonal quality of care, evaluate the technical quality of processes of care, determine most errors of omission or commission, or assess the appropriateness of care.

Various attempts have been made in recent years to enrich administrative databases with more clinical-relevant information. For example, measurement of quality of care would be enhanced if data on fatality rates could be case-adjusted (based on clinical background data) and if in-hospital case-fatality rates could be compared with rates derived from the national mortality statistics.

Achieving such improvements, will require linking databases. Because of rapidly evolving information technologies, this is technically, feasible. As discussed in the next sections, numerous efforts are shaping the future, particularly the introduction of electronic health records (EHRs) and unique patient identifiers (UPIs). Adoption of UPIs is being heavily debated in many countries for privacy reasons, although there is general consensus that such linkages are essential for constructing indicators of the quality and safety of care. Countries that have a UPI in place, such as those in Scandinavia, have a far greater capability for quality measurement. Thus, the expectation is that the definition, content, and scope of administrative data will change dramatically over the next several years. With improved recording and increased possibilities to link up medical records with registries and administrative databases, the possibilities to measure quality of care would also be enhanced significantly.

In this context, the OECD's Health Committee endorsed the advice of the HCQI Expert Group to promote the introduction of UPIs and coding of co-morbidities and diagnoses at hospital or nursing home admission. Moving forward, however, will require agreement over standards related to diagnoses, procedures, and other non-numeric clinical information to permit cross-country comparability.

Broader impediments to the introduction of ICT

ICT would seem to be an essential tool for improving health care quality and enhancing value for money given its capacity to facilitate data collection and the management and manipulation of large data files. The diffusion of ICT in the health care system to date has been, however, limited in comparison with that in other sectors of the economy in OECD countries. Moreover, adoption in health care has not diffused evenly through the health care market.

Currently, the most mature ICT applications are in the financial and administrative domains. Computer programmes to improve the efficiency of hospital business operations such as accounting, claims processing and records storage have been available since the early 1960s. Digital reporting of laboratory and radiology results is also well established in many countries. In comparison, adoption of applications aimed at improving the quality and timeliness of patient care has been slow. Cost and operational issues, such as payroll management and the search for efficiency gains, not clinical needs, have driven most investment in ICT in health care. The average community hospital, and even some large medical centres lack information technology enhancements intended to improve the efficiency of care and patient flow, inform clinical decision making, reduce medical errors and enhance provider-to-provider and provider-to-patient communication (IOM, 2006).

A significant body of literature has recently emerged that addresses the possible barriers to adoption of ICTs in the health care system (see, for example, Taylor *et al.*, 2005; and Scott *et al.*, 2005). Uncertainty about true costs, benefits and experience associated with these technologies appears to be a major barrier. These systems are expensive, and the investment is great both initially and on an on-going basis. Although the financial risk will vary according to the level and scale at which investment is made, the case for a return on investment cannot always be made clearly. A particular problem is the disconnection between who pays for and who benefits from ICTs. The analysis to date points to market failure and the need for incentives or regulatory policy changes.

In addition to the financial risk, there are great social and behavioural risks. The diverse nature of participants in the health care sector and the fragmented nature of health care systems are significant factors in the disappointing levels of adoption of ICTs. Care is often delivered by a variety of independent physicians and other providers working in a broad spectrum of settings. Making the most of information systems will require re-engineering systems and the evolution of organisational models towards integrated health care approaches and open sharing of information, knowledge, and experience. There are, however, strong institutional, financial, and cultural barriers to moving in this direction. At the local level, there is no financial reward for improved clinical information exchange among health care entities that regularly act as business partners providing care to a common set of patients.

Appropriate mechanisms for the adoption of standards and interoperability must also be established in order to exchange clinical information on common patients for treatment purposes (Ash and Bates, 2005). While health care organisations have access to an ever increasing number of information technology products, linkage remains a serious problem. The challenge of standardising information capture, given today's varied, proprietary, vendor-related, and often innovative approaches, remains a tremendous task despite recent public and private sector efforts (Waegemann *et al.*, 2002).

Using ICT for quality improvement: the opportunities

While quality measurement and reporting systems can produce data for accounting and research pruposes, they can also be used in a variety of ways to directly motivate performance improvements. For example, public disclosure of performance data is becoming increasingly common in a number of OECD countries. Another approach being tested in both public and private sectors is to tie provider compensation to a standardised set of quality-related performance indicators. Linking compensation to conditions that need improvement and are credible quality measures has proven particularly successful in primary care since general practitioners (GPs) are not easily persuaded to undertake change until they are presented with data and see for themselves the gaps between best practices and actual medical care delivered in their office.

Programmes which have adopted this so-called pay-for-performance (P4P) approach generally feature quality targets consisting of prevention-oriented, process-based measures for a number of chronic conditions. These targets reflect the high health payoffs of some types of preventive care and the high concentration of expenditures among persons with chronic conditions (Khunti *et al.*, 2007). Although no formal studies have yet to clearly answer this issue, early results from the implementation of P4P programmes in the United States and the United Kingdom indicate that payment policies linked to quality indicators can strongly influence how both the institutional provider (hospitals, health systems) and individual providers (physicians and other health professionals) deliver medical care.

Pay for performance itself is not a new concept in health care. Managed care organisations and other payers have been offering providers financial incentives to achieve productivity and efficiency targets for well over 20 years (Conrad and Christianson, 2004). The recent wave of P4P programmes, however, focus, in some cases exclusively, on quality of care. This reflects the belief that improvements in clinical quality will mean healthier patients and healthier patients, ultimately, will translate into long-term cost savings.

A defining feature of P4P programmes is the ability to reliably measure the provider's performance and quality of care reliably. Consequently, a major concern among providers participating in P4P programmes is the validity of the data used (Bokhour *et al.*, 2006). In addition, reporting requirements can be labour intensive and time consuming. Moreover, expertise is needed to analyse data, to hypothesise causes, and to devise improvement strategies. Most physician offices lack these systems and expertise. Thus, the mere creation of financial incentives will not close the quality chasm; programmes must concurrently develop supporting infrastructure and new capabilities for continuous improvement. As a result, most P4P programmes today directly link incentives with the adoption and use of ICTs at the point of care such as electronic prescribing or EMRs. High-quality ICT infrastructure can enhance the information-gathering capabilities of physicians and promote the electronic capture of laboratory, pharmacy, and other data sources necessary to expand the clinical measurement set from primarily process-oriented measures to outcome measures.

As part of its recent work on incentives for the adoption of health ICTs, the OECD has initiated a review of the better-known pay-for-performance efforts including the Integrated Healthcare Association's (IHA) P4P effort in California, and the National Quality and Outcomes Framework (QOF) in the United Kingdom (see Box 5.2). Similar incentive programmes have emerged and are being tested in both public and private sectors in many other OECD countries. For example, in Australia, the Practice Incentive Programme (PIP) was established to compensate physicians for fee-for service arrangements. It focuses on aspects that contribute to quality care in general practice. PIP has recently been expanded to include incentives for the use of bona fide electronic prescribing software and for use of an on-site computer to send and receive clinical information. In the Canadian province of Alberta, the Physician Office System Programme was established in 2004. It provides GPs with financial assistance, change management support, and training programmes to adopt ICTs for quality improvements in primary care. A similar programme was recently launched in British Columbia.

The English QOF programme has raised considerable international interest because it is both a pay-for-performance and pay-for reporting incentive scheme. It provides one of the clearest examples of how incentives can be put in place for both quality measurement and quality improvement. Without a doubt, high-quality ICT infrastructure and almost universal computerisation in primary care have been critical to its successful implementation. QOF is measured by QMAS, a national IT programme developed by the National Health Service's (NHS) Connecting for Health. QMAS ensures consistency in the calculation of quality achievement and disease prevalence, and is linked to payment systems. Data used to calculate clinical quality indicators is extracted from the individual GP clinical systems and sent automatically to QMAS monthly. The information is aggregated to the practice level.

Box 5.2. The UK National Quality and Outcomes Framework

The Quality and Outcomes Framework (QOF) was introduced in the United Kingdom as part of the new General Medical Services (GMS) contract on 1 April 2004. It is a voluntary annual reward and incentive programme for all GP surgeries in the United Kingdom.

The QOF includes four domains, each of which consists of a set of measures (referred to as indicators) against which practices can score points according to their level of achievement. They are as follows:

- *Clinical domain*: 80 indicators across 19 clinical areas (*e.g.* coronary heart disease, heart failure, hypertension);
- *Organisational domain*: 43 indicators across five organisational areas – records and information; information for patients; education and training; practice management and medicines management;
- *Patient care experience domain*: consisting of four indicators that relate to length of consultations and to patient surveys;
- *Additional services domain*: consisting of eight indicators across four service areas including cervical screening, child health surveillance, maternity services, and contraceptive services.

In 2004-05 physicians were scored against 146 performance indicators, with clinical quality accounting for more than 50% of the total. Each point earned had a financial bonus associated with it, and GPs stood to achieve additional compensation amounting to 30% of their salary. This represented a 20% increase in NHS's budget for GPs.

A year after introduction, QOF appears to have made a difference in the quality of patient care in two out of the three conditions that had been routinely monitored both before and after the introduction of incentives (asthma and diabetes). Results for 2004 show that GPs greatly exceeded projections of their performance and achieved a mean of 91% compliance with clinical guidelines. This result may also be partly attributed to the multiple interventions that preceded QOF such as the development of national guidelines for major diseases, a process called Clinical Governance, and a national inspection process.*

QOF also made a significant difference on the recording of coronary heart disease-related quality indicators and prescribing (mean absolute increase of 17.1%). On the other hand, there were only moderate increases in the attainment of cholesterol and blood pressure control among patients with stroke. And differences according to gender and income appear to have persisted in some components of care; for example, more affluent patients tended to have larger increases in recording of quality indicators. (McGovern *et al.*, 2008; Simpson *et al.*, 2006).

It is probably still too early to judge the final outcomes of QOF. A longer period of study may be required to capture significant improvements across all populations, particularly the most deprived who may be less willing to seek advice for their condition.

More recent studies continue ,however, to document improvements in quality of primary care in the United Kingdom (*e.g.* Khunti *et al.*, 2007) though, as previously noted, none can adequately address the relative importance of the QOF incentives compared to other quality improvement activities.

In the longer term, the new contract seems likely to change the behaviour of GPs as demonstrated for other similar schemes implemented in the United States (Beaulieu *et al.*, 2005). However, in the light of the substantial costs of the new contractual framework, countries intending to introduce similar changes should carefully assess the information requirements.

* There has been some controversy over the utility and cost of the programme, as some felt that many doctors may have been improving on quality of care in any case. This was impossible to judge *ex ante* as there were few indicators to assess GP performance in a systematic way prior to the introduction of the new contract.

There is no patient-specific data within QMAS. For example, although QMAS will capture practice-aggregated information on patients with coronary heart disease and practice-aggregated information on patients with diabetes, it is not possible to identify, analyse, or cross-link data from patients with both of these conditions. Organisational, access, patient experience, and additional service indicators are entered by the practice directly into QMAS via a web browser linked to NHSnet.

QMAS is not a comprehensive source of data on quality of care in general practice. Within the clinical domain, QOF only covers conditions affecting a minority of patients and only some aspects of the care for such patients. Even so, it provides valuable clinical information on these conditions on a scale previously unavailable. Over time it will generate a baseline against which to measure future levels of improvement. It can also complement other ongoing data collection efforts across general practices.

Linking health data across settings: the key challenges

Electronic data collection can facilitate patient care and measurements of provider's performance and also enhance the efficiency of surveillance, population and outcomes research. By reducing the amount of time needed to collect secondary data from individual patient charts, the availability of electronic data permits analysis of large sample. Moreover, in principle, ICT could also make available more complete and accurate data by linking health data about individuals longitudinally, across multiple settings, and from multiple sources. For example, data linkage could enable identification of factors such as hospital re-admission rates that may underscore specific health or quality issues.

There are several challenges in moving from paper records to electronic reporting. Paper records often lack the detail necessary for population-based studies. There is also little incentive for physicians to include additional information in these files. Furthermore, when supplemental data are entered, it is often done in a non-systematic manner.

Electronic reporting today is also hampered by lack of interoperability, the ability of systems to exchange information accurately and effectively. Areas of deficiency include issues of medical vocabulary, common identifiers, coding and data exchange. Thus, even when automated, data tend to be held in silos defined by legacy systems, organisational walls, or other boundaries. Disparate user information needs and existing (paper and electronic) source systems where the data reside represent core challenges to data integration.

Data security and privacy of personal health data represent the most acute issue in the dissemination of ICT applications. Decisions on how health care organisations handle their digital information environment can, therefore, profoundly affect the uptake of ICT for health care purposes. There are a variety of technical solutions to protect patients. For example, in the Netherlands, patients can completely opt out of participating in the electronic exchange of their health information. (In that case, this information is not recorded in any registry and cannot be accessed in an emergency.) They can also request the provider to conceal or mask discrete data items by withholding authorisation or by requesting the masking or concealing of specific information at the local level. They can mask or restrict access to their data by data element; by user or category of users; and by context. In the Canadian province of British Columbia, as further discussed in Box 5.3, individuals can mask their entire prescription record by having the pharmacist attach a keyword to the record. Thus, the main challenge for decision makers is creating a smooth interface between privacy policy, legislation and technological requirements.

The purpose and scope of privacy protection must be clear; unclear policies may have unintended perverse consequences. Although health care organisations have a strong interest in maintaining privacy and security, they must also balance this interest against the need to ensure that information can be retrieved easily when required for care. The cost of implementing some privacy protections has come under criticism (McCarthy *et al.*, 1999), as has their potential impact on employer-sponsored disease management programmes (Washington Business Group on Health, 1999), patients' family members (Pimley, 1999) and medical research (Vukadinovich, 1999). Legislation relating to privacy of patient information may limit the availability of quality data that is required to conduct formal evaluations of potentially beneficial ICT applications (Love and Sullivan, 2004), and this, in turn, may impact on the technical and clinical effectiveness of the resource in question.

Pharmaceutical information systems: PharmaNet in British Columbia (Canada)

The linkage problems discussed above can be at least partly overcome by putting an integrated health information architecture in place at an early stage. The Linked Health Database, housed at the Centre for Health Services and Policy Research in British Columbia (BC), is a good example. This database is among the richest data resources in the world for applied health services and population health research. It covers the entire population of BC, over 4 million residents. The data integrates medical claims, health service records, population health data, and census statistics, making it possible to link administrative records anonymously at the individual level. Researchers can thus trace the experience of a group of individuals over time and across health programmes. Pharmaceutical data holdings have been, however, limited until now.

Through linkage with Pharmanet (see Box 5.3) the database will soon enable future research into key areas of pharmaceutical policy, and improve the collection of system-wide patterns of pharmaceutical use among BC residents. It may also be used to understand the dynamics that influence pharmaceutical expenditures, permitting management of pharmaceutical financing in a more efficient and equitable manner. In addition, it can permit the examination – in an evidence-based manner for the entire province – of how the population responds to periods of rapid change in the health care system, or how they are affected by modification to pharmaceutical pricing policy.

Box 5.3. Pharmaceutical information systems: the opportunities

In the face of escalating and unsustainable expenditure growth for drugs in the 1980s and early 1990s, BC PharmaCare, the public drug plan in British Columbia, began a concerted effort to manage pharmaceutical expenditure better (Morgan *et al.*, 2004). In 1994, the BC Ministry of Health set up the Therapeutic Initiative (TI), a university-based advisory body of academics and health professionals, to assist with drug coverage decisions. An information system known as PharmaNet was established In September 1995 and today operates throughout the province, linking over 900 pharmacies into a centralised set of data storage systems supporting dispensing, monitoring, and claims processing for over 3 700 pharmacists throughout BC.* Currently, all prescription medications dispensed by pharmacies in British Columbia must be recorded on PharmaNet.

PharmaNet includes data on:

- patient drug profiles, including all drugs dispensed, reported drug allergies and clinical conditions;
- patient demographics which include the personal health number, name, address, gender, and date of birth;
- drug information for pharmacists, patients, and drug interaction evaluation; and
- claims information including eligibility, coverage, and deductibles.

The four main objectives of PharmaNet are to *1)* prevent the prescribing of harmful combinations of prescription drugs, *2)* increase cost-efficiencies, *3)* prevent multi-doctoring by prescription drug users, and *4)* provide fast, interactive access to patient information and personal health numbers.

Considerable emphasis has been placed on confidentiality. PharmaNet users sign confidentiality agreements before being granted access and provide unique identifiers when logging into the system. Patients can place a keyword on their profile to mask the data, and can also limit access to those individuals with whom they share the keyword.

* Over 38 million claims are processed through PharmaNet annually, with a financial impact budgeted in excess of CAD 1.13 billion dollars in 2007-08.

Conclusions

The examples presented in this chapter illustrate the potential of ICTs to contribute to quality measurement and active quality improvement, both of which can enhance value for money spent on health. Computerisation, unique patient identifiers, and linkage between databases can make it possible to chart patients' complex itineraries through health care systems and pinpoint areas to enhance system performance in terms of both costs and clinical outcomes.

Electronic records offer many opportunities, particularly to evaluate healthcare interventions and their quality at practice level. However, as also confirmed in a recent study by the Commonwealth Fund (Fowles *et al.*, 2008), evaluators must carefully select indicators and understand where weaknesses in data quality may lie. The current quality of data within these records sets limits on what may be achieved. Measures that translate established quality indicators may be perhaps the easiest to transfer into electronic health records. These measures usually have clearly defined specifications. And as the QOF example illustrates, attempts to enhance data gathering at practice level are likely to be successful only if there is a clear incentive and benefit to GPs and their patients.

Linking databases using unique patient identifiers holds the potential for huge gains in clinical and health services research. However, as the level of detail increases, so do issues of data confidentiality. Encryption and other technologies offer scope for protection of both patient and doctor identities. Privacy policies, however, must be clear and ensure the confidence of the general public that this highly personal information will not fall into the wrong hands.

Notes

1. Work is currently underway to establish an additional set of internationally comparable data including indicators on patient safety, mental health care, and primary care using, to a large extent, administrative data bases.

2. Screening rates for breast cancer and cervical cancer are often assessed through surveys, particularly in countries where no national screening programmes exist. Smoking rates are also established through population surveys, often in combination with other methods to validate the self-reporting.

Bibliography

Ash, J.S. and D.W. Bates (2005), "Factors and Forces Impacting EHR System Adoption: Report of a 2004 ACMI Discussion", *Journal of the American Medical Informatics Association*, Vol. 12, No. 1, pp. 8-12.

Beaulieu, N.D. and D.R. Horrigan (2005), "Putting Smart Money to Work for Quality Improvement", *Health Services Research*, Vol. 40, No. 5, Pt. 1, pp. 1318–1334.

Bokhour, B.G. *et al.* (2006), "Incentive Implementation in Physician Practices: A Qualitative Study of Practice Executive Perspectives on Pay for Performance", *Medical Care Research and Review*, Vol. 63, No. 1, Suppl., pp. 73S-95S.

Conrad, D.A. and J. B. Christianson (2004), "Penetrating the 'Black Box': Financial Incentives for Enhancing the Quality of Physician Services", *Medical Care Research and Review*, Vol. 61, No. 3, pp. 37S-68S.

Fowler, F.J. (2002), *Survey Research Methods,* Third Edition, Sage Publications, Thousand Oaks, CA.

Fowles, J.B., J.P. Weiner and K.S. Chan (2008), *Performance Measures Using Electronic Health Records: Five Case Studies*, The Commonwealth Fund, New York.

Donabedian, A. (1988), "The Quality of Care. How Can It Be Assessed?", *Journal of the American Medical Association,* Vol. 260, No. 12, pp. 1743-1748.

Fisher, E.S. and J.E. Wennberg (2003), "Health Care Quality, Geographic Variations, and the Challenge of Supply-Sensitive Care", *Perspectives in Biology and Medicine,* Vol. 46, No. 1, pp. 69-79.

Institute of Medicine (2000), *To Err is Human: Building a Safer Health System*. National Academy Press, Washington, DC.

Institute of Medicine (2001), *Crossing the Quality Chasm: A New Health System for the 21st Century*, National Academy Press, Washington, DC.

Institute of Medicine (2006), *Hospital-Based Emergency Care: At the Breaking Point*, National Academy Press, Washington, DC.

Khunti, K. *et al.* (2007), "Quality of Diabetes Care in the UK: Comparison of Published Quality-of-Care Reports with Results of the Quality and Outcomes Framework for Diabetes", *Diabetic Medicine*, Vol. 24, No. 12, pp. 1436-1441.

Lazarou, J., B.H. Pomeranz and P.N Corey (1998), "Incidence of Adverse Drug Reactions in Hospitalized Patients: A Meta-Analysis of Prospective Studies", *Journal of the American Medical Association* Vol. 279, No. 15, pp. 1200-1205.

Love, T. and F. Sullivan (2004), "Confidentiality, Clinical Governance and Research in the Community", *Informatics in Primary Care*, Vol. 12, No. 1, pp. 1-2.

McCarthy, D.B. *et al.* (1999), "Medical Records and Privacy: Empirical Effects of Legislation", *Health Services Research*, Vol. 34, No. 1, Pt. 2, pp. 417-425.

McGlynn, E.A. *et al.* (2003), "The Quality of Health Care Delivered to Adults in the United States", *New England Journal of Medicine,* Vol. 348, No. 16, pp. 2635-2645.

McGovern, M.P. *et al.*(2008), "The Effect of the UK Incentive Based Contract on the Management of Patients with Coronary Heart Disease in Primary Care", *Family Practice*, Vol. 25, No. 1, pp. 33-39.

Morgan, S., K., Basset and B. Mintzes (2004), "Outcomes-Based Drug Coverage in British Columbia", *Health Affairs*, Vol. 23, No. 3, pp. 269-276.

OECD (2004), *Towards High-Performing Health Systems*, OECD Publishing, Paris.

Pimley, D. (1999), "Maine Experience Shows Potential Snag as Public Grapples with Patient Privacy", *BNA Health Law Reporter*, Vol. 8, No. 5.

Pirmohamed, M. *et al.* (2004), "Adverse Drug Reactions as Cause of Admissions to Hospitals: Prospective Analysis of 18,820 Patients", *British Medical Journal*, Vol. 329, pp. 15-19.

Scott, J.T. *et al.* (2005), "Kaiser Permanente's Experience of Implementing an Electronic Medical Record: A Qualitative Study", *British Medical Journal,* Vol. 331, pp. 1313-1316.

Schuster, M. E., E.A. McGlynn and R.H. Brook (1998), "How Good Is the Quality of Health Care in the United States?", *The Milbank Quarterly*, Vol. 76, No. 4, pp. 517-563.

Simpson, C.R. *et al.* (2006), "Effect of the UK Incentive-Based Contract on the Management of Patients with Stroke in Primary Care", *Stroke*, Vol. 37, No. 9, pp. 2354-2360.

Taylor, R. *et al.* (2005), "Promoting Health Information Technology: Is There a Case for More Aggressive Government Action?", *Health Affairs*, Vol. 24, No. 5, pp. 1234-1245.

Vukadinovich, D.M. and S.S. Coughlin (1999), "State Confidentiality Laws and Restrictions on Epidemiologic Research: A Case Study of Louisiana Law and Proposed Solutions", *Epidemiology*, Vol. 10, No. 1, pp. 91-94.

Waegemann, C.P. *et al.* (2002), *Healthcare Documentation: A Report on Information Capture and Report Generation*, Consensus Workgroup on Health Information Capture and Report Generation, Medical Records Institute, Newton, MA.

Wennberg, J.E. (2002), "Unwarranted Variations in Health Care Delivery: Implications for Academic Medical Centres", *British Medical Journal,* Vol. 325, pp. 961-964.

Chapter 6.

The Impact of User Charges in Health Care

By Peter C. Smith
Professor of Health Policy, Imperial College Business School, London

This chapter examines current reliance of OECD countries on cost sharing and user charges in health care. It then looks at some European policy innovations and reviews some important results from the RAND health insurance experiment in the United States using variable levels of user charges. The chapter concludes with comments on the future role of user charges in developed health systems.

Introduction

Most health care is directed at individual patients and seeks to improve the duration and quality of their life. It is, therefore, feasible to charge patients a fee for their use of health care. Indeed it is worth recalling that, until recently, doctors in all countries relied mainly on patient fees to provide their income. It was only in the latter half of the twentieth century that socialised medical care became widespread in developed countries.

User charges in health care serve two broad purposes: to finance the health system and to send signals to patients who would otherwise face a zero price for access to health care. Developed countries do not rely to any great extent on charges as a significant source of financing. However, there has been a persistent concern with the dangers of what is referred to as moral hazard in health care (Zweifel and Manning, 2000). That is, in the absence of direct prices, patients may use health care when it is not warranted. Moreover, given the power of doctors to influence patient behaviour, moral hazard might be exacerbated by supplier-induced demand, particularly in systems where doctors' incomes rely directly on attracting high levels of business (McGuire, 2000).

What is known about the use of user charges and their effects on health care use and health status? This chapter first examines the extent to which OECD countries currently rely on user charges in health care.

[1] It then describes some European policy innovations, and outlines some important findings from the RAND health insurance experiment with variable levels of user charge in the United States. The chapter ends with some comments on the future role of user charges in developed health systems.

User charges in high income countries

Early experiments with subsidised health care in countries such as Germany and the United Kingdom were aimed predominantly at improving the health of low-income workers and the military. These arrangements evolved gradually into the systems of universal health insurance coverage and low user charges now in place in most OECD countries. Figure 6.1 shows the current pattern of private health care financing in those countries that report data to OECD, underlining the heavy reliance on public funds, in the form of tax or social insurance revenues.

Direct user charges (also referred to as out-of-pocket payments) account for between 10% and 20% of revenue. Most of the other private expenditure category referenced in Figure 6.1 relates to voluntary private insurance. In particular, in countries such as Ireland and France, patients are, in principle, liable for quite high user charges. However, many citizens take out voluntary private health insurance to secure protection from out-of-pocket payments.

Figure 6.1. Private expenditure as a percentage of total health expenditure, 2005

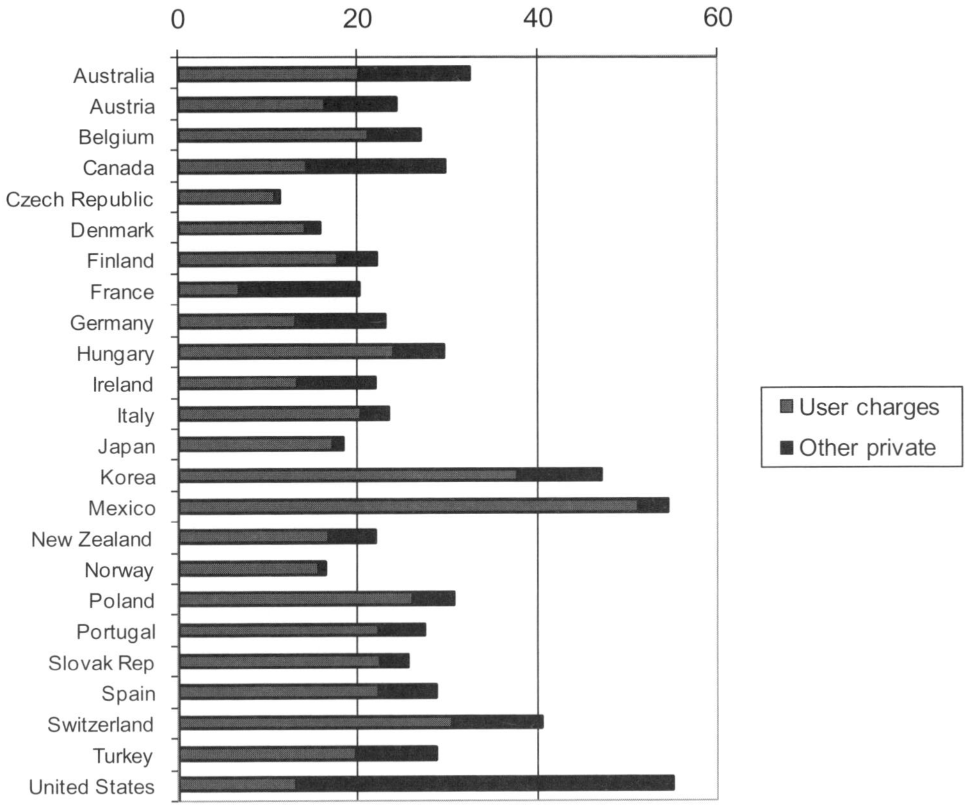

Source: OECD (2004), *OECD Health Data*.

Figure 6.2 shows trends over time in selected countries in use of out-of-pocket payments, as a percentage of total health expenditure. Although there is no discernible pattern in these trends, the absolute value of direct patient payments for health care generally increased over the period 1980-2005, because health care expenditure in total increased sharply in most countries as a proportion of the total economy.

Figure 6.2. Trends in out-of-pocket as a percentage of total health expenditure, 1980-2005

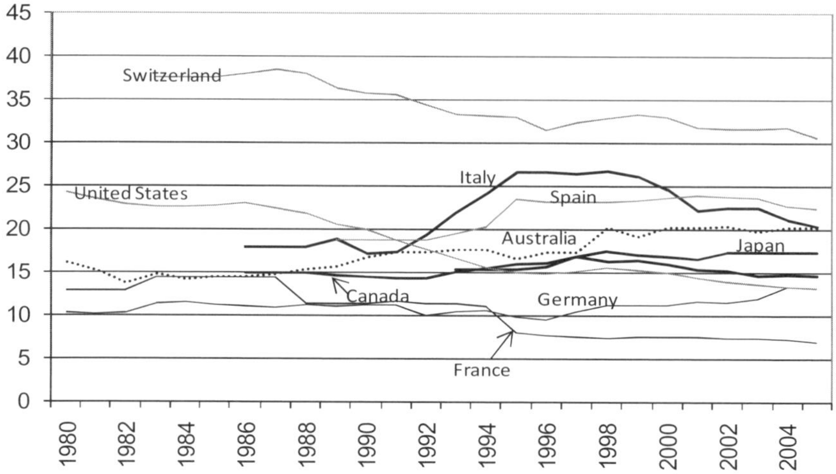

Source: OECD (2007), *OECD Health Data*.

When examining the economic implications of imposing user charges for health care, it is important to keep in mind the intense political passions they often generate. For example, Eversley (2001) relates the fraught history of charges in the UK National Health Service, the imposition of which, in 1951, led to the resignation of the health minister, hastening the demise of the Labour government. Even where charges have been imposed, exemptions have become widespread. For example, in 2004, prescription charges in England accounted for income of GBP 446 million. But only 8.9% of prescriptions directly attracting the full charge of GBP 6.20 (House of Commons, 2005). The vast majority of prescriptions are exempt from charges on grounds of age (young and older people), sickness (certain chronic conditions), maternity, or low income. This is typical of experience in many countries.

It is also worth noting that many lower income countries do not offer patients the protection from charges enjoyed in high-income countries. Indeed, worldwide over 50% of health care financing is in the form of out-of-pocket payments. High reliance on user charges is inescapable in low-income countries in which a governmental or private insurance capacity is infeasible, and generally leads to poor health system performance. It is therefore important to emphasise that the discussion here is relevant mainly for developed health systems.

Developments in Europe

Western Europe countries have traditionally sought to model their health systems on the principle known as solidarity. This implies universal coverage, and contributions to the financing of health care according to ability to pay, irrespective of age or level of sickness. User charges appear to contradict the principle of solidarity. Yet, with the inexorable growth in expenditure on health care, there has been growing interest in imposing some modest charges (Robinson, 2002).

In general, more recent efforts to impose user charges have not raised much revenue. Indeed in some circumstances the sums involved are outweighed by the collection costs. Rather, the main purpose of these innovations has been to encourage patients to use the health system to better purpose, by discouraging treatment when benefits are small and incentivising efficient use of services when it is justified, some examples are:

- moderating use of drugs,
- encouraging use of cheaper generic drugs,
- discouraging multiple consultations of alternative doctors,
- directing patients through gatekeeper physicians,
- encouraging the use of less costly or higher quality preferred providers, and
- encouraging early discharge of patients from hospital.

Most of these initiatives have been directed at cost containment. Many other experiments in a similar vein could be envisaged, such as charging patients for outpatient visits, but offering a full or partial rebate if the first appointment is honoured (in order to discourage people from failing to keep appointments). Moreover, user charges could, in principle, be used to encourage healthier behaviour on the part of patients. For example, one could envisage a scheme of exemption from charges if a patient complies with a course of treatment in its entirety. A few European innovations up to 2005 are described below.

Sweden was one of the first of the traditional public sector systems to experiment with small user charges across a wide range of health services. Children and young people are generally exempt, and the maximum annual liability for charges has traditionally been set at quite a low level (EUR 90 in 2001). Such modest charges appear to have been generally accepted as reasonable. They did, however, result in reduced utilisation amongst low-income patients, and a concern that equity of access may be compromised (Andersen *et al.*, 2001).

The Netherlands relies on a system of competitive social insurance, and has traditionally repudiated use of direct charges. However, since 2005, insurers have been allowed to offer premium discounts to insurees who make no use of hospital inpatient facilities in the preceding year, in effect imposing a retrospective charge for hospital use.

Starting in 2004, Germany experimented with a EUR 10 charge for the first appointment with a doctor in each three-month period, up to an income-related maximum. Initial findings suggested little change in the proportion of patients making some contact with a doctor, but some reduction in the average number of contacts made. Because there was no evidence of a disproportionate impact on the poor or sick, an early evaluation was therefore cautiously optimistic that the reform is reducing intensity of use without harming patients (Gericke *et al*, 2003; Grabka *et al.*, 2005).

In France, since January 2005, patients have been charged a small fee (EUR 1) for each consultation, intervention and test. Also, for adults not suffering a long-term illness, a supplemental charge was made for consulting a specialist without the endorsement of a nominated gatekeeper physician (*médecin traitant*). This charge was variable, but for a basic consultation, the fee was about EUR 7. French patients have traditionally enjoyed unfettered access to health care professionals, so this was a tentative attempt at moderating demand for specialist care. So that it could have the intended effect, policy makers sought to prevent inclusion of these new charges in the traditional complementary insurance used by many French people (Bellanger and Mossé, 2005).

A form of user charge that is widespread within Europe arises from the use of so-called reference prices for drugs with examples in Germany, Italy, Spain and Sweden. Under this regime, pharmaceuticals with similar properties are grouped into discrete clusters. Patients are reimbursed at a fixed rate for all drugs within a cluster, if they choose a more expensive drug; they must pay the difference between the drug price and the reference price out of their own pocket. The intention is to encourage use of cheaper generic replacements of branded drugs (Kanavos and Reinhardt, 2003). The impact of reference pricing on demand and health outcomes has yet to be satisfactorily evaluated.

Some countries in eastern Europe have experienced especially severe problems with financing health care, and have therefore experimented with more radical approaches to user charges, especially where there was a tradition of informal payments to doctors and other professionals (Lewis, 2002). A particularly ambitious scheme of diagnosis based reimbursement was developed in the Slovak Republic. A national tariff for reimbursing providers was to be set for all interventions, according to diagnosis. Patients would then be reimbursed for a proportion of the costs of treatment, depending on the diagnosis group. The proportion reimbursed depended on the estimated benefits and costs of treatment, with full reimbursement for 33% of diagnoses. This scheme was consistent with the prescriptions of the economic theory known as optimal commodity taxation (Smith, 2005). However, the experiment was never fully implemented, and a change of government led to its abandonment in 2006.

Evaluating user charge experiments

There is little reliable evidence on the impact of user charges on the utilisation of health care and the health of patients in developed countries. The major exception is the celebrated RAND health insurance experiment, under which over 2 000 US patients were randomly assigned to one of four charging regimes over an extended period (Newhouse, 1993). One group of patients enjoyed complete freedom from charges, while those at the other extreme were charged 95% of fees for virtually all care, up to a maximum annual catastrophic liability of about USD 6 000 at current prices.

Some results from the experiment are summarised in Table 6.1. They show consistent reductions in utilisation across all types of health care as the charges became more severe. For example, physician consultations varied from 4.55 per annum amongst those incurring no charges, to 2.73 amongst those in the highest charging scheme, a reduction of 40%. However, with one major exception, evaluation of the experiment did not detect any material variations in health outcomes associated with charging. Researchers have therefore concluded that, for most of the population, charges succeeded in encouraging less profligate use of health care without serious health consequences. The one important exception was the finding that charging had a seriously adverse effect on those who were both poor and suffering from poor health. The RAND evaluation estimated that for this disadvantaged group there were a wide range of serious consequences, in spite of some cost subsidy for low-income families. For example, when charges were imposed, hypertension was less well controlled in this group, to the extent that the annual likelihood of death rose by approximately 10% (Newhouse, 2004).

Table 6.1. Annual use and spending per person in the RAND health insurance experiment

Coinsurance (%)	Visit rates		Admission rates		Spending (USD 2003)	
	Number	Standard error	Number	Standard error	Amount	Standard error
0 (free care)	4.55	0.17	0.128	0.0070	1,377	58
25	3.33	0.19	0.105	0.0070	1,116	51
50	3.03	0.22	0.092	0.0166	1,032	58
95 (high deductible)	2.73	0.18	0.099	0.0078	946	47

Source: Newhouse, J.P. (2004), "Consumer-Directed Health Plans and the RAND Health Insurance Experiment", *Health Affairs*, Vol. 23, No. 6, pp. 107-113.

It has proved much more difficult to evaluate the consequences of user charges where there is no experimental design, and researchers have had to resort to econometric analysis to infer their impact. Such analyses in other countries appear to corroborate the RAND results. For example, results from Belgium suggest a distinct impact of charges on demand for home visits and office visits by general practitioners, except amongst older or disabled patients (van de Voorde *et al.*, 2001).

Conclusions

The question thus arises: what is the most appropriate role for user charges in a modern health system? Experience in high-income countries suggests a persistent tension between the equity goal of assuring universal access to health care and the efficiency goal of assuring frugal use of health services. In short, unless carefully designed, user charges designed to curb excessive demand amongst the general population could have ruinous financial or health consequences for a relatively small number of poor people with health problems. It is therefore important to view the design of user charges within the broader objectives and institutions of the health system as a whole.

With the notable exception of the United States, there is a general consensus that public funding of tightly regulated healthcare delivery should lie at the core of the modern health system. However, there is also a growing trend towards the use of small but symbolically important user charges. These new charging initiatives are intended both to influence specific aspects of patient behaviour and act as a signal of preferred behaviour. Moreover, they may help reassure the taxpayer that patients are being encouraged to use the services they pay for responsibly. Charges have not hitherto been used to generate significant amounts of revenue for developed-country health systems.

Moreover, notwithstanding the modest nature of the experiments described above, in the medium term, the accelerating pace of technological innovation and the inexorable rise in patient demand may require a more fundamental rethinking of user charges. Hitherto, developed countries have been able to ensure that most mainstream interventions are included in their statutory package, allowing policy makers to claim that coverage is comprehensive. However, there is growing evidence that such a policy may become financially unsustainable, and that policy makers may have to resort to increased use of explicit rationing of some aspects of health care (Coulter and Ham, 2000).

Under this scenario, the central policy problem is to decide which health care technologies should be subsidised from public funds. A policy of user charges then flows naturally from the choice of the subsidised treatments. Once the public package of care is chosen, patients would still be free to purchase the remaining unsubsidised interventions at market prices, or to purchase complementary private insurance to cover such interventions. This was the essence of the Slovak experiment.[2]

The scope of the statutory package should be determined by the public's willingness to pay the necessary taxes - in particular, the willingness of the healthy and the rich to subsidise the sick and the poor (de Graeve and van Ourti, 2003). It is therefore essential that the package is of high quality, so that richer people do not choose to use private care in preference to publicly subsidised care. If quality is poor, widespread resistance to paying the taxes required to finance the public package may arise, making the public system unsustainable.

Increasingly, health technology assessment agencies such as the British National Institute for Health and Clinical Excellence (NICE) are being asked to evaluate new technologies, and to issue associated clinical guidelines. Although a daunting technical undertaking, such agencies could, in principle, be given the expanded mission of recommending the entire scope of the publicly subsidised package. Charges (partial or total) would then be paid by patients on interventions that fall outside the chosen package. Indeed, one could envisage that, if a technology fails the country's cost-effectiveness criterion, agencies such as NICE could nevertheless include it in the public package but only at partial coverage of costs. The patient would then be asked to fund the difference between the NICE price and the provider's price.

An important aspect of any charging policy is the choice of patient groups to be exempted from charges. Indeed, one could envisage that for some patient groups, there may be a case for introducing negative user charges (subsidies) to encourage increased use of treatments with especially high personal or social benefits, such as smoking cessation therapies. In practice, the issue of exemptions has proved problematic for policy makers, and it has rarely been feasible to introduce charges without making exemptions for vulnerable groups. For example, successive UK governments have introduced exemptions for prescription charges on the grounds of age (young and old), health needs (an apparently arbitrary selection of conditions) and income, resulting in a very low proportion of patients being liable for charges. When introduced carelessly, exemptions pervert the intended economic signals. Yet equally, the evidence from RAND and other experiments is that at least some disadvantaged patients will suffer catastrophic financial or health effects without some system of abatement of charges.

In summary, the publicly funded health system of the future should include the following features:

- an explicit set of interventions subsidised by public funds (the health basket), the choice of which is guided by the criterion of cost-effectiveness;
- the size of the health basket determined by the willingness of the population to pay the necessary taxes;
- charges (partial or total) paid by patients on interventions that are not deemed cost-effective;
- those able and willing may purchase voluntary (complementary) insurance to protect against such charges;
- no compromises are made on the quality of publicly funded health care;
- a carefully crafted system of exemptions from charges exists to protect the very poor; and,
- small charges are permitted even on some fully subsidised interventions, as signals of preferred behaviour.

This system may at first glance appear unattractive compared to the widely adopted principle of comprehensive health care, free of charge to all users. Yet it will be infeasible to adhere to that principle indefinitely, as the scope of health care technology increases inexorably and the limits to public funding sources are reached. In that case, the proposals set out here offer policy makers a framework for making the hard choices that follow. It will take political courage to implement such explicit rationing, but the alternative may be to reduce steadily the scope and quality of statutory health care by stealth, and reduce the widespread commitment to solidarity on which publicly funded health care relies.

Notes

1. This chapter is based on a paper prepared in 2006, and some of the country experiences described are somewhat out of date. They should be considered a basis for discussion rather than a comprehensive description of the current situation.

2. From an economic perspective, the choice of interventions in the public package should be guided mainly by the expected health benefits they bestow in relation to costs (Smith, 2006). Equity concerns should in my view be tackled not by the health care system, but by the tax system used to finance the public package. However, if political considerations demand that the package should be skewed in favour of diseases of the poor, then this does not affect the general principle of explicit definition of the package.

Bibliography

Andersen, R., B. Smedby and D. Vågeröc, (2001), "Cost Containment, Solidarity and Cautious Experimentation: Swedish Dilemmas", *Social Science & Medicine*, Vol. 52, No. 8, pp. 1195-1204.

Bellanger, M. and P. Mossé (2005), "The Search for the Holy Grail: Combining Decentralised Planning and Contracting Mechanisms in the French Health Care System", *Health Economics*, forthcoming,

Coulter, A. and C. Ham, (2000), *The Global Challenge of Health Care Rationing*, Open University Press, Maidenhead.

Eversley, J. (2001), "The History of NHS Charges", *Contemporary British History*, Vol. 15, No. 2, pp. 53-75.

Gericke, C., M. Wismar and R. Busse, (2003), "Cost-sharing in the German Health Care System", Discussion Paper, Department of Health Care Management, Technische Universität Berlin, Berlin.

Grabka, M., J. Schreyögg and R. Busse, (2005), "Verhaltensänderung durch Einführung der Praxisgebühr und Ursachenforschung - eine empirische Analyse", DIW Discussion Paper No. 506, Deutsches Institut für Wirtschaftsforschung, Berlin.

de Graeve, D. and T. van Ourti, (2003), "The Distributional Impact of Health Financing in Europe: A Review", *The World Economy*, Vol. 26, No. 10, pp. 1459-1479.

House of Commons (2005), "Hansard 27 Jan 2005: Column 561W", The Stationery Office, London.

Kanavos, P. and U. Reinhardt (2003), "Reference Pricing for Drugs: Is It Compatible With U.S. Health Care?", *Health Affairs*, Vol. 22, No. 3, pp. 16-30.

Lewis, M. (2002), "Informal Health Payments in Central and Eastern Europe and the Former Soviet Union: Issues, Trends and Policy Implications", in E. Mossialos, A. Dixon, J. Figueras and J. Kutzin (eds.), *Funding Health Care: Options for Europe*, Open University Press, Buckingham.

McGuire, T. (2000), "Physician Agency", in J.P. Newhouse and A.J. Culyer (eds.), *Handbook of Health Economics,* Elsevier, Amsterdam.

Newhouse, J. (1993), *Free for All? Lessons from the RAND Health Insurance Experiment*, Harvard University Press, Cambridge MA.

Newhouse, J.P. (2004), "Consumer-Directed Health Plans and the RAND Health Insurance Experiment", *Health Affairs*, Vol. 23, No. 6, pp. 107-113.

OECD (2004), *OECD Health Data*, OECD Publishing, Paris.

OECD (2007), *OECD Health Data*, OECD Publishing, Paris.

Robinson, R. (2002), "User Charges for Health Care", in E. Mossialos, A. Dixon, J. Figueras and J. Kutzin (eds.), *Funding Health Care: Options for Europe*, Open University Press, Buckingham.

Smith, P. (2005), "User Charges and Priority Setting in Health Care: Balancing Equity and Efficiency", *Journal of Health Economics*, Vol. 24, No. 5, pp. 1018-1029.

Smith, P. (2006), "Public Packages of Health Care alongside Voluntary Insurance", in A. Preker, R.M. Scheffler and M. Bassett, M. (eds.), *Private Voluntary Health Insurance in Development: Friend or Foe?*, World Bank, Washington, DC.

van de Voorde, C., E. van Doorslaer and E. Schokkaert, (2001), "Effects of Cost Sharing on Physician Utilization under Favourable Conditions for Supplier-induced Demand", *Health Economics*, Vol. 10, No. 5, pp. 457-471.

Zweifel, P. and W. Manning (2000), "Moral Hazard and Consumer Incentives in Health Care", in J.P. Newhouse and A.J. Culyer (eds.), *Handbook of Health Economics*, Elsevier, Amsterdam.

OECD PUBLISHING, 2, rue André-Pascal, 75775 PARIS CEDEX 16
PRINTED IN FRANCE
(81 2009 17 1 P) ISBN 978-92-64-07420-0 – No. 57045 2009